Divine Chinese Cuisine

Divine Chinese Cuisine

100 Recipes • 70 Vegan Options
No Gluten, Dairy, Seafood, Nuts, Dye or MSG

Lillian Pearl Bridges & Stephen A. Lesefko

LOTUS INSTITUTE PRESS
www.LotusInstitute.com

Published by
Lotus Institute Press
Seattle, WA • USA
www.LotusInstitute.com

Published in the United States of America

First published in 2020

Print Edition ISBN 978-1-7341150-0-0
eBook ISBN 978-1-7341150-1-7

Photos by Alex Lesefko and Stephen A. Lesefko

Book design and production by Barbara Tada
www.pixelgardendesign.com

For more information about programs and classes visit:
www.LotusInstitute.com

*This book is dedicated
to Kingway and Lea Lowe.*

*Our first cooking teachers and our
inspirations for this cookbook.*

Contents

CHAPTER 6
Cold Plates & Salads

CHAPTER 7
Dim Sum Favorites

CHAPTER 8
Savory Bites

CHAPTER 9
Wraps & Rolls

CHAPTER 10
Chinese Vegetables & Sweets ... 175

Introduction

Chinese people talk about food more than they talk about anything else. In Northern China, people greet one another with the question, "Have you eaten yet?" And, even if you have, they will want to feed you. Because I grew up in a home with a Chinese Mother, I realized early on that Chinese people love to eat. You could easily say they live to eat.

Chinese Food is one of the great cuisines of the world and I was lucky to be born into a family of wonderful cooks and had my palate educated to the taste combinations of exquisite Chinese food. Small differences in the amount of the same ingredients or changes in the shape or size of an ingredient makes a huge difference to the finished dish. I learned many secrets of Chinese cooking that most restaurant chefs won't teach you, and I am happy to share them with you in this set of three cookbooks.

My Chinese Grandfather, Kingway Lowe, was an extraordinary chef from the Shandong Province on the Northeast coast of China. He swears that he is a descendant of Confucius, but apparently everyone from this region claims that same distinction. Because he carried strong Confucian values, I believe that this philosophy of cooking and eating played a part in the way that he cooked. He favored simplicity of flavors, fine knife skills and the freshest and highest quality of ingredients. If you have ever seen the film *Eat Drink Man Woman*, you would have a good idea about how he cooked. He never had less than 12 dishes on the table and sometimes there were as many as 16!

He got his love of cooking from his Mother, who loved to cook so much that she would invite beggars off the streets of Jinan to eat because she cooked too much food for the family! My Grandfather was a brilliant man who paid for his education by working as a cook. He was the first in his family to get a University Degree in Shanghai and he cooked at a Chinese fraternity when he went to the University of Michigan to earn his Master's Degree. When he married my Grandmother, who came from an extremely wealthy Shanghai banking family, he learned that she did not cook, as girls of that class rarely did. She had a very refined palate, so he learned to make all of her very favorite Shanghai foods and Imperial Banquet dishes to keep her happy.

During World War II, my Grandfather opened a three-story restaurant in Shanghai. He had previously been a University President, but he was in danger because of his American connections and education. Owning a restaurant had always been a dream for him and while he was able to run it, it was quite successful. The first floor was for takeout food, the second floor was for casual dining and the top floor was for banquets. He was saddened when he was forced to close it.

When he was finally able to come back to America, he settled in Los Angeles and started a successful sweater company. He still loved cooking and he cooked every day that he could. He became known at the Los Angeles Farmer's Market as "Mr. Fava Bean" because he bought them so often and picked them so carefully. The entire family gathered together every weekend and eating was the focus of the day. I was so privileged to learn how to cook from my Grandfather. I've never had better Chinese food in my life, except for a few times when I have perfected one of his dishes. And that means it tastes just like his.

He taught me how to prepare everything for Chinese cooking and I spent many hours being one of his Sous Chefs. I started off picking off the heads and tails of bean sprouts to make perfect "silver needles." I took the strings off thousands of green beans and pea pods. And, I have pleated so many dumplings (boiled Jiaotze and pan fried Guotie) that I can make them blindfolded. Then I learned knife skills and how to cut ingredients and they had to be exactly the same size! Over time, I was given more responsibility for the preparation of food, although I was never allowed to cook a complete dish. I watched my Grandfather carefully because he never measured anything, I had to learn more about what seasonings and spices he used and in what proportion and combination rather than how many teaspoons, tablespoons or cups of ingredients the recipes contained. He educated my palate so well that I learned how good Chinese food is supposed to taste. He coached me to understand that the different dishes should incorporate the Five Flavors – salty, sour, bitter, sweet and savory/pungent to create a balanced meal.

We rarely went out to eat because my Mother was also a wonderful home cook and she made Chinese food nearly every night. When we did go out, it would be for Dim Sum and I loved all the dumplings. Dim Sum restaurants are crowded places with the constant clatter of trolleys carrying a variety of little plates of dumplings and pastries that you can choose by pointing to what you want. It is also called Yum Cha, which means that you drink Tea with these snacks to help digest the fatty nature of these little plates of delicious food.

I still love Dim Sum, but I can't go to Dim Sum restaurants any more because I have developed a lot of food allergies and intolerances. I have had to become very cautious about what I eat and it's getting harder to eat out. I quiz waiters at restaurants about the hidden ingredients in their food and read all labels at grocery stores very carefully. I mostly cook at home, and I wanted to recreate wonderful Dim Sum treats and Chinese dishes that were free of most of the major allergens. That was the inspiration for this cookbook series.

I've tried to remain true to my Chinese roots and have primarily shared recipes based on my Grandfather's cooking and my Mother's dishes, but I and my sons grew up with modern American Chinese food. The Chinese diaspora meant that local ingredients were used and tastes were adapted so that dishes like Chop Suey or General Tso's Chicken were created that are not found in China but are still delicious. In fact, many of these dishes are being brought back to China and are becoming quite popular at Western-style Chinese restaurants. The point is that Chinese cooks have always adapted to the ingredients on hand wherever they live. And Chinese food at the core uses lots of vegetables with a small amount of protein, with a variety of seasonings and sauces. It is a healthy cuisine and I am attempting to make it even healthier for all of those people, like me, who have food allergies and intolerances.

My oldest son, Stephen, helped me extensively in writing this cookbook so it's his cookbook too. He started cooking with me from a young age and you will see his hand in the development and testing of every single recipe. I would create a recipe or he would, and then we would each test it again before we made it several more times together, just to be sure it was right.

Luckily, Stephen is a master of Sauces and started recreating all the important ones so that we don't miss the mass produced ones at all because the homemade ones are so much better. He is always encouraging me to go bolder and stronger in my use of seasoning – particularly in the use of Chiles, since he loves the MaLa flavors of Sichuan food. He is amazing with a wok and much more willing to take risks when it comes to seasoning than I am.

He previously worked as a Chef at an Asian Restaurant and created all their special sauces, some of which we've included in this cookbook. I treasure his palate, as he is so good at detecting nuances of flavor and adding that extra something that is the sign of a great chef. Sometimes, he reminds me so much of my Grandfather! Professionally, he is a Winemaker and I am so happy that he also loves to cook as he is carrying on a family tradition. My son Alex has a very refined palate as well, and he was my number one taste tester and editor. I so appreciate his honesty about what dishes worked and which ones didn't! They were the primary photographers for this book, as that is a talent I don't have!

Both my daughters-in-law – Kelsey and Allison were also so helpful. They were our other primary taste testers. I thank them for their amazing team spirit, since they had to taste things over and over again. Kelsey helped me create the recipes involving sweets, and Allison, who is from China, helped us keep the tastes authentic, especially in dishes from her hometown. Both of them are very artistic and were very involved in the food styling. All of their suggestions and help were invaluable and I am so grateful!

A big thank you goes to Hannah Shearer for her thorough and thoughtful editing, and to Lizzy Scott for her early editing and assistance in creating the Divine Chinese Pantry. Thank you to Etch Haring as well, for coming up with the name of this cookbook series. A special thank you goes to Deirdre Courtney and Sabine Wilms for their advice and support. I am so grateful for Kelly Harrington's many contributions in getting this cookbook ready to publish. And, I am forever indebted to Barbara

Tada for her wonderful graphic design skills in laying out this cookbook and I so appreciate her refined design aesthetic.

So, in this series of cookbooks, we are giving you many of our family's secrets about how to make great Chinese food, and here is one of the first ones: you have to love to cook! And if you are cooking for people you love, your family and your friends, the food will taste even better because you will infuse it with love. I learned this from my Grandfather. One of my favorite memories is of my Grandfather taking me with him into the kitchen of a new Shanghai restaurant owned by a friend of my Uncle's that had just opened up in Los Angeles. My Grandfather asked to meet the head chef and then asked him several questions (in Chinese). As we walked back to our table, I asked my Grandfather what he had asked. He told me that he asked the chef if he loved to cook because he never ate at a restaurant if the food was not made with love because he would get a stomachache. And, for me that is the most important secret of good cooking.

We are sharing family recipes and recipes that we have created out of our love for the Divine Cuisine of China. We hope you enjoy making and eating these Chinese dishes that come from our family that are free of many troublesome ingredients, yet still full of authentic Chinese flavor!

Lillian Pearl Bridges
Seattle, WA USA

CHAPTER 1

Chinese Philosophy of Food

A well-known Chinese saying: *"Eating is as important as the sky,"* shows that the Chinese love and value food beyond measure. For those of you readers who are not Chinese, you may not be aware of how much the topic of food shows up in normal conversations. One of my Chinese friends in Singapore considers the Chinese to be obsessed with food because you often see Chinese people talking about their next meal even before they have finished the previous one!

Food is considered essential to Chinese culture, possibly because it is a country that was so prone to famine and has always had the need to feed so many people. So, figuring out how to grow enough to feed them all was a priority. That's why the Chinese will eat anything edible and that breaks all kinds of Western food taboos. They can make amazing meals out of small amounts of meat or doufu (tofu) and combine it with lots of vegetables and create sauces with a drizzle of this and a drop of that. A few dishes and a bowl of rice is the epitome of Chinese home cooking.

This frugality with ingredients has created a cuisine that is very healthy and varied and the balance of the diet is very different from the Western emphasis with meat as the star of the main course. Rice is the staple grain (except for in the North where there is Wheat and Millet) and is present at almost every meal. In addition, the Chinese may eat so many vegetables and they have developed many cooking methods and techniques that make them one of the great cuisines of the world. Chinese Chefs can take the same ingredients and by varying the size of the ingredients and the proportion of the ingredients can create distinctly different dishes. Chinese food and cooking have evolved over the centuries into a highly refined art.

The Food Regions of China

China is a vast country with many different regional styles of cooking. Each region has a wide variety of different foods and spices available that have helped inspire countless creative dishes and unique tastes. Although these regions used to be more isolated in the past, the signature dishes found in China's many provinces have now spread far and wide around the world and are the basis for putting together this cookbook.

Cantonese food is probably the most well-known Chinese food outside of China and comes from the Southeastern region of the country and includes Hong Kong. This is because the largest and first groups of emigrants to the West came from this region and brought their style of cooking with them. Cantonese food is known for its delicate flavors and lightly steamed or stir-fried meats and vegetables and their sweet sauces. This style is particularly known for their desire to maintain the food's original flavor. Dim Sum is one of the most famous exports from this region.

Shanghai was one of the wealthiest areas of China and the traditional food was considered very refined and their banquet foods were legendary. Shanghai food has always stressed the importance of freshness of the food, along with the all the sensory aesthetics involved in presentation of the food, including color, aroma as well as emphasizing pure and natural flavors. Therefore, they do not use a lot of seasoning that can overwhelm subtle tastes. They are known for their braised foods and Xiao Long Dumplings.

Shandong cuisine was very important in the history of China, as it influenced the Imperial Cuisine of Peking (now Beijing) and was the home of Confucius. Harmonious flavors are mainly emphasized. As such, food here is generally known for its freshness and the varied cooking styles and cooking with a lot of Garlic, Onions, Scallions and only a little Chili and Ginger. They use a lot of Vinegar and Salt and they take care to preserve the color and taste of the food. Their dishes are known for their light aroma, richness and freshness. They use many more grains than other regions

The food from Hunan is known for being Hot, Pungent, Sour and Salty. They use a lot of Chili Peppers in many forms, along with Shallots, Garlic, Vinegar and Citrus fruit. Hunan food is actually the hottest food in China. They love their savory, spicy food and they are fond of dry, hot food.

Sichuan Cuisine comes from a province of Southwestern China. It is the most popular cuisine of China and has become increasingly popular around the world. It is known for bold flavors – the complex hot and spicy Ma La taste that includes the numbing quality of Sichuan Peppercorns. They use a lot of seasonings and the food often has thick gravy. They use Hot Chili Oils as a frequent seasoning. Sichuan Cuisine is pungent, hot and fragrant.

The Northwest Shaanxi Province has a strong Mongolian Influence and the Xinjiang Region in the far West of China has a strong Silk Road influence. These areas border the desert and have a diverse population of other ethnic groups. Their cuisine uses a lot of Lamb, Mutton and Beef due to their large Muslim population. Wheat is the primary staple and they eat more dairy products than other parts of China. They have fewer fresh vegetables, so they eat a lot of preserved, dried and pickled vegetables.

The Chinese Diaspora has taken Chinese food all across the world, with changes made in every location to create new forms of Chinese food. The Chinese have always adapted to the local conditions and use locally grown vegetables and fruits. Chinese food in some places, like the U.S., is barely recognizable in China. Restaurants that feature dishes like Chop Suey and Sweet and Sour Pork are catering to a different palate and the food is sweeter and less subtle in flavor than traditional Chinese food. The same thing has happened in England, Australia and New Zealand, where some of the dishes served would mystify someone from China. Some areas of the world, like Singapore, have kept many of the regional cuisines such as Teochow food completely traditional. And the Chinese people that migrated to Southeast Asia have an influence that can be seen clearly in modern Thai, Vietnamese and Indonesian cuisine in their stir-fry dishes and sauces. These days in the US, there are more and more restaurants serving Chinese food that is authentic and sometimes surprising to Westerners. And, most recently, American style Chinese food has returned to China and has become increasingly popular among the youth there.

While most Chefs in big restaurants in China are men, women have always been encouraged to cook as well, particularly in the home. In fact, during the Soon Dynasty, female Chefs were revered. These days, both men and women cook Chinese food and if they don't cook, they frequent the many Chinese restaurants on a regular basis. It is true that if a Chinese restaurant is full of Chinese people, it is going to have very good food. Chinese patrons demand the best!

The Quality and Presentation of Ingredients

The most important thing for all Chinese cooks is freshness of the ingredients. This is why they keep their fish swimming in tanks before cooking them and examine all the fruit and vegetables carefully before buying them.

Chinese food is almost always cooked, except for fresh fruit, and they serve very few raw salads. Most of their salads usually consist of lightly sauced and blanched vegetables, as the Chinese believe that cooked food is easier to digest and of course, is safer to eat. Soup is served at most meals and is considered important for warming up the stomach, as is hot tea. They even start the day with Congee or Jook, which is rice cooked with a lot of water or broth and served with bits of meat, egg, peanuts and pickles, etc.

Cooking most Chinese food involves cutting all ingredients into relatively small pieces, which makes it easier to use chopsticks, but also makes it easier to chew and digest the food. Some food is hacked into large pieces and others are cooked as whole as possible. When cutting, most of the ingredients in the same dish will be cut the same size. Having good knife skills is a sign of a great Chinese Chef. The size of the ingredients also affects the taste and texture of a dish and the cooking technique of stir frying most likely evolved from using straw fires to cook over, which made it necessary to cook fast before the fire went out. This has since evolved into an art form.

My Grandfather used to say that first the food must smell good and one of the tricks he used that many chefs use is to drizzle just a little bit of toasted Sesame Oil to give foods a wonderful fragrance. Then it must look good to the eyes. The Chinese love combining different colors in each dish and sprinkle garnishes like bits of Green Onion, Cilantro, Red Pepper and/or Sesame Seeds to liven up the presentation. Then of course, the dish must taste good! They believed that when it tasted good, it was even better for you.

The Magic of Tea

The Chinese favor Tea above all other beverages. The legend is that the Chinese Emperor Shen Nong was waiting at a campsite to drink a cup of hot water when the dried leaves of a Camellia Sinensis bush were blown by the wind and landed in the pot, flavoring it in a delicious way and giving it a wonderful aroma. The Emperor was enamored by this new drink and found it very refreshing. It soon spread throughout the land and became an intrinsic part of Chinese culture.

Tea is now the most popular beverage in the world, after water. And, a Chinese meal, especially Dim Sum would not be the same without Tea. In fact, the Cantonese name for Dim Sum is *Yum Cha* which means to drink Tea while you eat snacks. The ancient Chinese considered Tea to be a medicinal beverage that aided in the digestion of fats. Modern science has proven that Tea is a drink with many health benefits with each type of Tea having different protective and health enhancing qualities.

Chinese Tea can be White, Yellow or Green based on how the leaves are dried. These Teas have a mild grassy taste. Or, the Tea Leaves can be partially oxidized as in Oolong, which has a lovely fragrance and has qualities of both Green and Black Tea. Or, Tea can be fully oxidized, as in Red Tea and fermented for a long period of time for a Black Tea like Pu'er, which has a very robust taste. Teas may also be flavored with Jasmine or Osmanthus flowers, which are very popular options. Other Teas made from different plants and flowers, like Chrysanthemum are actually Tisanes. Chrysanthemum Tea is a very popular option, especially in the summertime. It is considered a very cooling beverage and is often served with Dim Sum.

Some of the health benefits that have been attributed to Tea include: lowering inflammation; reducing fat and cholesterol; regulating blood pressure; enhancing dental health; reducing fatigue; helping to make bones stronger; enhancing blood vessel elasticity; and may be possibly anti-bacterial. Tea may also protect against Cancer and Alzheimer's. As you can see, Tea is truly a magical drink and luckily it tastes good too! We recommend serving all Chinese food with Tea.

The Divinity of Food

Chinese Food is all about preparation, as the actual cooking time is fairly quick for most dishes. While it may seem that there is a lot of preparation involved in making Chinese food, it is actually an exercise in mindfulness. There is something very calming about peeling and chopping vegetables and gathering spices. I consider it to be a kind of moving meditation. My Grandfather once told me that the most expensive dishes in restaurants were often the fastest to make. The reason why they cost so much is that they demanded the full attention of the Chef. This means that cooking keeps you in the present moment, which can make cooking a somewhat spiritual experience.

I was also taught by my Grandfather to *Eat the Sun,* which means to eat fruits and vegetables at their peak of ripeness so that you could absorb the highest amount of nutrients. You are then being fed by one of the most powerful energies of the Cosmos. This also means that animals can sometimes digest the sun better than people do and that's why some people need to eat meat and others are fine being Vegetarians or Vegans. It's why foods like honey, or meat and butter from free-range cows who eat grass grown in the sun, or free-range chickens and their eggs are so much healthier. And sun-ripened fruits and vegetables just taste so much better. The Chinese consider all food to be a divine gift.

Eating good food is about gathering Ling – the magical energies of the Universe that enhances life. In Chinese Medicine, food is one of only two substances – the other being breath - that can be transformed into Qi or Life Force Energy. Breathing the right way is called *Breathing the Moon.* Both Eating the Sun and Breathing the Moon are a part of Daoist Alchemy. And, Alchemy can only occur when there is fire. In this case, the fire comes from the emotion of Joy. This means, that in order to transform food into Qi, it is required that you truly enjoy your food in order to get the maximum benefit from it. So, eat what you love and remember to eat the sun, because it means you will be healthier.

CHAPTER 2

The Divine Chinese Pantry

The Divine Chinese Pantry

Aduki, Adzuki, Azuki Beans – *see* Red Beans

A Choy/AA Choi – a type of Taiwanese Lettuce with a taste and texture much like the leafy part of Romaine Lettuce. Romaine can be substituted.

Agar Agar – a jelling agent, similar to Gelatin, but is derived from Seaweed and is considered a vegetarian/vegan substitute for Gelatin.

Allspice – this is the small rounded dried fruit of a West Indian Tree and is called Allspice because it tastes like a combination of several spices. It is occasionally used in Chinese cooking.

Amaranth Greens/En Choy – This is a leafy green vegetable with small leaves, used in Chinese cooking as an ingredient in stir-fries and soup.

Apples – a sweet edible fruit from an Apple Tree. It is rounded in shape with a thin skin of yellow to red and a crisp, juicy flesh that ranges from tart to very sweet.

Asparagus – the young shoots of the flowering, fern-like Asparagus plant that is eaten as a vegetable. The Chinese use Asparagus mostly in stir-fry dishes and it is usually cooked very briefly to retain some crunchiness.

Baking Powder – a dry, lightly acidic, chemical leavening agent. Some Gluten Free brands include, *Argo*, *Bob's Red Mill*, *Hain* and *Rumford*.

Baking Soda – a dry chemical leavening agent used with acid to create lift in baked goods. The Chinese also use it in small quantities as a meat tenderizer.

Bamboo Shoots – these are the edible sprouts of many Bamboo species. They are used as a vegetable in Chinese Cooking. They cannot be eaten raw, so they must be cooked first. They are most easily found canned but can also be found dried. They are lightly fibrous and crisp and add texture to many Chinese dishes.

Bananas – the edible fruit of the Musa genus of flowering plants with large leaves. The fruit is botanically considered a berry. It has a yellow peel and the fruit inside sweet, soft and somewhat starchy.

Bay Leaves – the leaves of the Bay Laurel tree. They are used dried as a seasoning and have a distinctive resinous flavor and aroma that they impart to food. The Chinese use them in spiced broths and in pickles. They are not meant to be eaten and should be removed from dishes before serving

Bean Curd – *see* Tofu

Red Beans, Azuki, Adzuki, Azuki – these are small, plump Red Beans that are cooked until soft that are used in a variety of sweet dishes, such as Red Bean Soup or they can be mashed into a sweetened paste to stuff dumplings and buns.

Sweet Red Bean Paste – mashed, cooked Red Beans that are sweetened with Sugar and mixed with either Oil, Lard or Ghee to make a filling for dumplings and buns, and as an alternative filling for Char Siu Bao.

Sweet Bean Sauce/Tian mian – a thick sweet sauce usually made from fermented Wheat and Soybeans. It is traditionally used with Roast Duck and as a sauce ingredient in stir-fry dishes. We have found one wheat-free version from *Master Sauce Company* in Taiwan, but it is hard to find, so we usually substitute Hoisin Sauce or Sweet Tamari.

Bean Sprouts – these are the sprouts of Mung Beans that are white with a small yellow seed head and a tapering root. They are a much-used ingredient in Chinese cooking. They are usually blanched when used in cold dishes and are frequently used in stir-fry dishes and as a filling for Eggrolls. Like all sprouts, they are considered very nutritious.

Bean Thread Noodles – *see* Glass Noodles

Beef – traditionally, Beef was not eaten much in China until recent times primarily because Oxen were considered working animals. However, it has become more and more popular in China and with overseas Chinese because of the availability of high-quality Beef. It is used most often in stir-fry dishes, but can also be found stewed, boiled, steamed and minced.

Beet Root Powder – Dried and powdered Beet Root. Used as a natural red food-coloring agent.

Salted Black Beans/Fermented Black Beans/Douchi – These are salted and dried Black Soybeans that are a favorite condiment in China. The fermentation process gives these Salted Black Beans a unique pungent and savory taste that is absolutely delicious! You can buy them in jars already made into a sauce, but we recommend that you buy a bag of the Salted Black Beans to keep in your pantry and use as needed. They keep for a long time and add a special flavor to so many dishes.

Bok Choy – leafy green vegetable with white, crisp stalks. It is a member of the Brassica family of vegetables and is used most often in stir-fry dishes.

Baby Bok Choy/Shanghai Bok Choy – this is a smaller version of Bok Choy with light green stems and darker green leaves. It is a tender vegetable that is less crisp than regular Bok Choy and can become very soft when cooked too long.

Bouillon – dehydrated Chicken, Beef or Vegetable Broth, usually made into cubes but can also be found powdered or in a paste form. It is used as a flavor enhancer and in Chinese cooking is often used in salad dressings. *We usually use HerbOx in America and Knorr in Europe.*

Bell Peppers – These are bell shaped sweet peppers that come in Green, Yellow, Orange and Red colors, which indicate various stages of ripeness. They are often used in stir-fry dishes and sometimes salads to bring in extra color.

Chinese Broccoli – *see* Gai Lan

Buddha's Hand Melon/Chayote/Mirliton Squash – a green gourd fruit that is shaped like a pear. It has a thin green skin with a large flat seed and a texture similar to Cucumber with a mild taste. When you turn it over, it looks like a closed fist, which gave rise to its Chinese name. It can be eaten raw or cooked.

Cabbage/Headed Cabbage – a round, smooth, green, densely leaved member of the Brassica family. This type of Cabbage has been used extensively by overseas Chinese, as a replacement for Chinese Cabbage, which was harder to find. It has now has become an important ingredient for Chinese cooking in the West. It is especially good cooked quickly in stir-fries because of its crunchy texture.

Chinese Cabbage/Celery Cabbage – *see* Napa Cabbage

Black Cardamom/Amomum tsao-ko – this is a large seedpod with a strong, camphor-like flavor. It is used primarily in braised meat dishes and spiced broths like hotpot.

Carrot – a root vegetable, usually orange, although there are yellow and purple varieties as well. The texture of a Carrot is crunchy and the taste is sweet. Carrots are a very versatile vegetable and can be cut in many ways. They are especially valued for adding color and texture to many Chinese dishes.

Cassava Flour – a Gluten Free, grain free flour made from Cassava or Yucca. In baking, it acts very much like Wheat flour and is a good one-to-one replacement. It is derived from the whole root, which is dried and ground. Although made from the same plant, it is not the same as Tapioca Flour.

Celery – a vegetable with long, thick, juicy and fibrous stems. Celery has a distinct slightly salty taste and aroma. It can be eaten raw and is often used in stir-fry dishes for its crunchy texture. Chinese Celery has thinner hollow stems, lots of leaves and a stronger Celery flavor. It is used primarily cooked in stir-fry dishes.

Chard – a leafy green vegetable with large white, red or yellow stems. It is a member of the Beet family and is highly nutritious. It is very much like Spinach with a subtler flavor and can be eaten raw in salads or cooked.

Chayote – *see* Buddha's Hand Melon

Chestnuts – the seed of the Chestnut Tree. It is encased in a hard, brown shell and needs to be roasted and peeled. Once cooked, the seed becomes starchy like a baked potato, with a slightly sweet and nutty taste.

Chicken – a very popular meat used in Chinese cooking. Chicken can be cooked in many ways and is used whole, ground, cut into parts or cut into small pieces for stir-frying.

Chicken Broth – this is pre-made Chicken Broth packaged in cans or cartons for convenience. We *like to use Swanson's Natural Goodness brand.*

Fresh Chiles – a fruit of the Capsicum family that varies in heat based on the variety. We used: Serrano, Jalapeño and Green Thai Bird Chiles and for Red Chiles, we used Red Jalapeño and Red Thai Bird Chiles.

Dried Red Chili flakes or whole Red Chiles – these are crushed Red Chiles and are typically used in large quantities in Sichuan and Hunan food. Most Chinese people enjoy using some Chili Oil or Chili Sauce on and in their food.

For authenticity, you can buy them from Sichuan online and they can usually be found in Asian grocery stores. But you can also use the more commonly found whole Chiles de Arbol or the Crushed Red Pepper Flakes, usually from Cayenne Chiles, that are commonly used as a Pizza topping. *We use the McCormick Organic brand for Stephen's Crispy Chili Oil.*

Chili Bean Sauce – a spicy, salty paste made from Broad Beans or Soybeans, Salt, Rice and various spices. Many Bean Sauces contain wheat, so read the label carefully. If you can't find one that is Gluten Free or without MSG, substitute Chili Garlic Sauce. *The brand Wan Ja Shan Formosa Chili Bean Sauce is Gluten Free, as are Ning Chi's Hot Soybean Paste and Fermented Chili Bean Sauce from Master Sauce Co.*

Chili Garlic Sauce – a sauce made from Garlic and Chilies with varying degrees of heat. We have a recipe to make this in this cookbook. But if you would like to buy it, the recommended Gluten Free types include, *Lee Kum Kee*, *Huy Fong Rooster Sriracha* and *Sambal Oelek,* and *A Taste of Thai.*

Chili Oil – this is made from infusing Red Chili flakes into a light tasting Vegetable Oil with other seasonings. It is an important condiment for Chinese food. We give you two recipes to make this at home, but if you would like to buy some at an Asian market, the recommended brands include: *La Yu*, *Lee Kum Kee*, *Dynasty* and *Kadoya Brand. The popular Lao Gan Ma Spicy Chili Crisp from China is delicious, but it does contain MSG.*

Chili Powder – this is made from dried and powdered Red Chilies. The various types can be very mild to very hot. We recommend Sichuan Chili Powder or the Korean Red Pepper Powder In either a fine or coarse grind.

Chinese Chives/Garlic Chives/Jui Cai – this member of the Allium family has long flat leaves and is used much like Green Onions in Chinese cooking. Although they smell strongly of Garlic when uncooked, they are mellowed by cooking and are delicious in dumplings and in stir-fry dishes.

Cilantro/Chinese Parsley/Coriander – a green leafy herb with an unusual taste that is used extensively as seasoning and garnish in Chinese cooking. Some people lack the gene that makes this herb taste good and for them, it can taste soapy. Those who love Cilantro, they describe the flavor as being fresh and like a combination of parsley and lemon, while also being a bit peppery. The stems, root and seeds of this plant are all edible.

Chinese Cinnamon/Cassia – a warming aromatic spice that is actually the bark of a tree that is sold dried and curled in sticks or ground. It can be used in both sweet and savory recipes.

Choy Sum – this is a green leafy vegetable from the Brassica family that has small yellow flowers. It is also known as Chinese Flowering Cabbage and has a mild taste similar to Gai Lan.

Cloves – these are the flower buds of an evergreen tree. They have a strong taste and are very aromatic. They are one of the ingredients in Five Spice Powder.

Coconut Aminos – this alternative to Soy Sauce and Tamari is made from fermented Coconut Tree Sap and Salt. It has an Umami flavor that is salty and a bit sweet, but it is lighter in color and flavor than Soy Sauce.

Coconut Milk – this is the white creamy liquid extracted from grated fresh Coconut. It has a high fat content and a mildly sweet taste. It is used to make Sweet Soup, Puddings, Coconut Jelly and Chinese Coconut Chicken Curry.

Coriander Seeds – these are the dried seeds of the plant known as Cilantro or Chinese Parsley and they have a lemony taste. They are used in soups and braises, and as an ingredient in Curry Powder. They are considered a warming and a medicinal spice in Chinese cooking.

Cornstarch – this is powdery flour derived from Corn and is used for thickening sauces and for coating for fried foods. It is used extensively in Chinese cooking and is valued because it keeps a sauce clear and allows the sauce to cling to the ingredients.

Cucumbers – this is a cylindrical berry of the Gourd family. It has a green skin and seeds in the center with a crisp and juicy texture and a mild, refreshing taste. It is a much loved ingredient in Chinese food and is used raw in salads and cold plates. It is also cooked in stir-fry dishes. Cucumbers are considered a cooling food and are particularly appreciated in the summer months or to tame the heat of hot chili. The types used in this cookbook include Slicing Cucumbers that have a thick green skin that must be peeled and the seeds should be removed; Japanese or Persian Cucumbers that are thin-skinned with small seeds – these can be smashed and eaten without peeling or deseeding; and English Hot House Cucumbers, which have a thin skin and small seeds and can be eaten whole. However, they have a milder flavor and will need more seasoning.

Cumin – the brown seed of a flowering plant in the Parsley family that is used as a seasoning. It looks very similar to Caraway and it has a distinctive flavor that is slightly smoky. It is an ingredient of Curry Powder and is used extensively in the Western areas of China.

Curry Powder – a mixture of various dried and powdered spices from India that were adapted by the British to make a commercial spice blend. Curry Powder usually includes: Coriander, Cumin, Turmeric, Ginger, Fenugreek and sometimes Red Pepper. Each individual brand also adds other spices. Curry Powder should be gluten free. *Our favorites brands are: Japanese S&B, Sun Brand Madras Curry Powder and McCormick, if you like your Curry mild.*

Daikon Radish – This is a large, white Radish grown in winter. It has a very mild taste and is very juicy. It is sometimes called Chinese Turnip and is used to make a savory cake, as a filling for dumplings and buns or for pickles. Daikon Greens are also edible and are sometimes used in stir-fry dishes.

Edamame – *see* Soybeans

Chinese/Japanese Eggplant – these are long, slender and light purple (Chinese variety) or dark Purple (Japanese variety). They have a relatively thin skin and fewer seeds, so they are less bitter than other kinds of Eggplant. Chinese Eggplant can be cooked in a number of different ways and is particularly good with strongly flavored sauces.

Eggs – Chicken, Duck and Quail Eggs are all used in Chinese cooking and are cooked in a variety of ways. They are considered nutritious and versatile ingredients. They are used boiled and marinated as Tea Eggs or Soy Sauce Eggs, they are scrambled and used in Mu Shu or Fried Rice, they are drizzled into soup; used as a binder for Meatballs; and are an important ingredient in baked goods. The Chinese also preserve Eggs in brine, as in Salted Duck Eggs or packed into minerals, as in Thousand Year Eggs or Century Eggs.

Gluten-Free English Muffins – these are a substitute for the Bai Ji Mo Sandwich Buns. Popular brands include: *Glutino, Canyon Bakehouse, Ener-G, Kinnikinnick Foods and Food for Life*

Fennel Seeds – the brown seed of the flowering Fennel plant. The seeds are small and have a grain-like appearance and a licorice-like taste. They are often used in Chinese braised dishes and are an ingredient in most Five Spice Powders.

Five Spice Powder – a mixture of five or more dried and powdered spices that usually include: Star Anise, Cloves, Chinese Cinnamon, Sichuan Peppercorn and Fennel Seeds. It is a commonly used Chinese spice blend that gives many dishes a unique taste.

Gluten-Free Flour Mixes – these are mixtures of several Gluten Free Flours including: White and Brown Rice Flour, Tapioca Starch, Cornstarch, Potato Starch, Millet Flour and Sorghum Flour. Several brands available include: *Arrowhead Mills, Better Batter, Bisquick, Bob's Red Mill 1 to1, Dove's Farm, Gold Medal. King Arthur Measure for Measure, Krusteaz, Manini's, Namaste, Pamela's Products. Our favorite is Cup4Cup, although this does contain Milk Powder as an ingredient.*

Our version of a basic Gluten-Free Flour Blend

> 1 cup White Rice Flour
> ¼ cup Brown Rice Flour
> ¼ cup Cornstarch
> ¼ cup Tapioca Starch
> ¼ cup Potato Starch (or Millet Flour or Sorghum Flour)
> 2 teaspoons Xanthan Gum

Gai Lan/Chinese Broccoli – this is a leafy green vegetable with blue-green leaves and an edible stem. It has a taste similar to Western Broccoli but is considered to be slightly more bitter. It is a popular Chinese vegetable and can be blanched, steamed or stir-fried and in this cookbook, it is also roasted.

Garlic – a plant in the Allium family closely related to Shallots and Onions. This flowering plant produces bulbs that are grown underground. Each bulb is made up of multiple individual cloves encased in a papery wrapper. It has a pungent taste and smell when raw that mellows with cooking. Garlic can be used whole, crushed, sliced or minced for cooking. Garlic is also dried and granulated, as well as being made into a seasoning powder. Garlic is considered one of three most important seasonings in Chinese Cuisine along with Green Onions and Ginger.

Ginger – the rhizome of a flowering plant that has a unique spicy taste and is considered a medicinal herb that is good for digestion. It is used extensively in Chinese Cooking and is said to take away the gaminess of meat. Older Ginger has a thicker brown skin that must be peeled before using (try using a spoon) while fresh Spring Ginger has a thin skin that can be eaten. Ginger is used sliced, slivered, crushed, minced and grated and it is considered an essential ingredient, along with Green Onions and Garlic in Chinese Cooking.

Glass Noodles/Bean Thread Noodles/Cellophane Noodles/Sai Fun – these noodles are made from Mung Bean Starch and are translucent and slippery when soaked in hot water or added to hot liquids. However, they become opaque white, puff up and become crispy when fried. They are used in Soups, Hotpots, as a filling ingredient in Dumplings and Spring Rolls and as a garnish.

Golden Syrup – a thick, sweet sugar syrup from England that is used in this cookbook to make Char Siu Sauce as a substitute for Maltose, which contains wheat.

Green Beans/String Beans – these are long, slender, green bean pods with beans that are still immature inside. Green Beans can be boiled, steamed or stir-fried.

Green Onions/Spring Onions/Scallions – these have a milder taste than regular Onions. Similar in shape to Leeks, but much thinner, they have a small white bulb and long green stems. They are used extensively in Chinese cooking in all manner of dishes and the green part is a favorite garnish. They are considered an essential flavoring ingredient along with Ginger and Garlic.

Chinese Ham – an air-dried cured leg of pork. Ham is considered a very important ingredient in Chinese cooking and is used to flavor stewed and braised foods and especially broths and soup. It can also be eaten cold as a meat plate. Chinese Ham is very salty and you need to use only a small amount for flavor. American-style Ham that is most similar to the Chinese kinds include: *Smithfield Virginia Ham and Country Ham and in Europe, you can substitute Jamon Serrano.*

Hoisin Sauce – A thick, sweet sauce traditionally made from Soybeans. It is considered an important condiment in Chinese cooking and is used for marinades, glazes and sauces. Most commercial brands are made with wheat so read the labels carefully. Our recommended gluten free options include: *Joyce Chen, Kikkoman, Lee Kum Kee, Wok Mei, Premier Japan, San J and Edward & Sons. We used Joyce Chen's and Kikkoman for the recipes in this book.*

Honey – a sweet, syrupy condiment made by bees. Used for glazing and sweetening many foods in Chinese cooking and also for beverages.

Jicama/Yam Bean/Chinese Potato – the tuberous root of a vine that is rounded with a light brown peel and a juicy, crisp white interior. It adds texture to Chinese dishes.

Ketchup – although it is not considered a traditional Chinese condiment, it was first created by the English based on Southern Chinese fish sauces. It has since become a standard Chinese ingredient and used as a sweet component in many sauces. Recommended gluten free brands include: *Heinz Organic, Hunt's, Annie's Natural, French's, Muir Glen Organic* and *Organicville.*

Lamb – this is a red meat mostly commonly eaten in the Northern and Western regions of China. It is considered a warming food.

Lard – this is rendered Pork Fat, the best of which is Leaf Lard, and is used in baking to make pastry and pie crusts flakier. Most Chinese pastries were traditionally made with Lard, but some bakeries now use Vegetable Shortening instead. However, Lard has been shown to be a healthy food, in moderation. When used in frying, it has a high smoke point.

Leeks – a member of the Allium family with long, thick, white to green stems that are actually thin layers of leaves. They have a mild Onion-like taste and soften with cooking. The white part of a Leek is considered most edible, whereas the darker green parts are used to flavor vegetable broth.

Lettuce – a green leaf vegetable with a mildly bitter taste that is primarily used in salads. The Chinese often use Lettuce leaves as a wrapper and even stir-fry it. The favorite type for Chinese cooking is Iceberg, due to its crisp texture, although other types may also be used, including: *Butterhead, Looseleaf – both Red and Green,* and *Romaine.*

Lotus Leaves – these are the large, fan-like dried leaves of the Lotus plant. When rehydrated, they are used as a wrapper for Sticky Rice or Fried Rice. Lotus Leaves impart the food it encases with an earthy fragrance, much like Tea Leaves and keeps the ingredients moist while they are being steamed.

Lotus Root – this is actually the stem of the Lotus plant and is used as a vegetable in Chinese cuisine. It has a brown skin and when peeled, it reveals white flesh that is crisp and juicy like a raw potato with round holes in it. It is very beautiful when sliced. It is cooked in a number of ways and is especially popular in banquet dishes.

Lotus Seeds – the edible round seeds of the Lotus flower, usually sold dried. When cooked, they have a starchy texture that is often sweetened to make a paste for Chinese pastries or they are used whole, crystallized with Sugar and made into candies. They are also used in soups and as an ingredient in Sticky Rice Wrapped in Lotus Leaves.

Mandarins/Tangerines/Clementines – this is a small fruit of the Citrus family. The flesh is juicy and sweet to sweet-tart and can be eaten fresh out-of-hand or used in sauces. You can also find canned Mandarin Oranges. The peel is also used as a flavoring in some Chinese dishes

Mango – a sweet tropical fruit that varies in color from green to yellow, orange, red and purple. Mangoes vary in texture from soft to firm to fibrous and they also vary in size, but all have a large oblong seed in the center. We like to use the Ataulfo Mango, which is yellow, as it is readily available.

Sweet Melon – a member of the Cucurbitaceae family that is actually a large, round berry. There is an outer rind that gives way to flesh that is soft and sweet and there are numerous seeds in the center. The Chinese usually eat Melons as a sweet treat or use them in desserts. In this cookbook, we use Honeydew and Cantaloupe.

Michiu – *see* Rice Wine

Millet – a small yellow seed that is naturally Gluten Free. It is an ancient grain of Northern China that was used as for porridge and is also ground into flour used for making flatbreads and noodles.

Mirin – a sweet Japanese Rice Wine, similar to Sake that is Gluten Free. It can be used as a substitute for Chinese Rice Wine, although it is usually sweeter.

Mu'er/Tree Ear/Wood Ear Mushroom – this is a Black Fungus that is grown in trees. It is sold dried in whole pieces or shredded and must be reconstituted in water. It has a crunchy and rubbery texture with very little flavor. In Chinese Medicine, it is said to be good for the blood.

Mung Beans – these are small green legumes that encase a light, yellow bean. They are sold dried with the peel on or off. The Chinese cook them peeled and use them for dessert soup or make them into a sweet paste to fill dumplings and buns. They are also ground into a starch to make Glass Noodles and they are sprouted.

Mung Bean Sprouts – *see* Bean Sprouts

Mushrooms – these are various types of edible fungi that have a cap, a stem and gills. They are used extensively in Chinese cooking and are often considered a meat replacement. They are valued for their Umami flavor and can be used either fresh or dried. Recommended types for this cookbook: *Button, Crimini, Enoki, King Oyster* and especially *Shitake Mushrooms.*

Chinese Mustard – a spicy condiment made from the seeds of the Mustard plant that is made into a paste with water. It is most often used in Chinese Cuisine as a dip for BBQ Pork or Egg Rolls. There are many brands of Chinese Mustard that can be purchased at the store, but it is simple to make at home with the recipe in this cookbook.

Mustard Powder – this is the powder ground from Mustard Seeds. It has a sharp peppery bite and is used to make Chinese Mustard. *We usually use Colman's.*

Napa Cabbage – a variety of Cabbage that originated in Northern China. This Cabbage is oblong in shape and has crunchy white stems and soft, light green crinkled leaves. It is a very important ingredient all over China and can be eaten raw, stir fried, in dumplings, in soups or made into pickles.

Nata de Coco – these are small, chewy, slightly fibrous, jelly-like cubes made from fermented Coconut Water. They add texture to desserts, like fruit salad and in this cookbook are added to Lychee Jelly.

Oil/Vegetable Oil – this is a liquid fat usually extracted from seeds that remains liquid at room temperature. Neutral or light tasting Vegetable Oils are best for Chinese food and when stir-frying look for ones that have the highest smoke point (flash point). While Peanut Oil is very popular in China, we use *Spectrum High Heat Safflower Oil*. Other Vegetable Oils with a high smoke point include: *Avocado Oil, Rice Bran Oil and Sunflower Oil. Canola Oil* can also be used, although it does have a lower smoke point and is better used lower temperature cooking or in salad dressings. *Olive Oil is not recommended for Chinese cooking unless it is Extra Light, as the flavor of Olive Oil is too strong for many Chinese dishes.*

Onions – a bulb vegetable from the Allium family with many crisp, juicy layers and a papery skin. Both Yellow and Red Onions are used in this cookbook. Onions have a strong smell and taste when cut raw, but they become sweet when they are cooked and very sweet when caramelized. They are considered a very important ingredient in Chinese cooking and they are used in a number of ways. They can also be cut into different sizes to match the size of other ingredients.

Oyster Sauce – this is a much loved and much-used condiment in Chinese cooking that adds a deep Umami flavor to Chinese dishes. Unfortunately, those with Shellfish allergies can't eat this sauce and the Vegan versions usually contain wheat. So, we have included a Vegan substitute for Oyster Sauce in this cookbook.

Pea Pods/Mange Tout – these are from a variety of Peas grown for their edible pod and come in two main varieties: Sugar Snap Peas are crisp, meaty and sweet – they can be eaten raw or cooked; Snow Peas are flat pea pods with minuscule peas inside. Both are usually eaten lightly cooked so that they remain crisp and are a favorite vegetable in stir-fry dishes.

Pepper – the dried fruit of a flowering vine, called a Peppercorn that is dried and used as a spice and seasoning. It can be used whole in soups or ground to release more of its flavor, which the Chinese consider hot and is the hot ingredient in Hot and Sour Soup. While the Chinese do use Black Pepper, they use even more White Pepper in their cooking, which is slightly milder in flavor.

Pineapple – a sweet to tart tropical fruit with a hard, spiky skin and yellow juicy flesh with a fibrous core. It is eaten fresh as a snack and is also canned for use in desserts.

Plum – a small rounded or oval stone fruit with dark purple or red skin and yellow flesh. The Chinese eat them out-of-hand or make them into Plum Sauce, which is served with fried foods and Duck.

Pork – this is the most popular meat in China and used extensively in Chinese cooking. It is a very versatile ingredient and can be cooked in many ways. It is also salted and cured as Chinese Bacon, Ham or Sausages.

Potato – a starchy root tuber that is rounded or oblong in shape and can be cooked in a number of ways. The outside peel can be brown, red, white or yellow and Potatoes come in variety of sizes. When peeled, the color of a Potato is generally an off-white or light yellow. The Chinese cook them as a vegetable, which leaves them crunchier and less starchy than in Western preparations.

Potato Starch – flour made from dehydrated Potatoes that is used in Chinese cooking for breading, and in this cookbook it is also used as an ingredient in Gluten-Free Flour Blends and to make Dumpling Wrappers

Rice Flour – a powdery white flour made from dried and milled long, medium or short grain Brown or White Rice. Rice Flour is used extensively in Chinese cooking for making Noodles and Wrappers and to coat food before frying. It is also used in this cookbook as an ingredient in Gluten-Free Flour Blends, Pastry and Dumpling Doughs.

Rice Noodles/Mai Fun – these are noodles of various widths made from Rice Flour that are usually Gluten Free, but be sure to read the label. The primary ingredients should be Rice Flour and Water. Sometimes Tapioca Starch or Cornstarch is added. They are used extensively in Asian cuisines and can be found fresh or dried.

Rice Vinegar – *see* Vinegar

Rice Wine – an alcoholic beverage made from fermented Rice. The most famous kind is Shaoshing Rice Wine, which unfortunately contains wheat. Look for the clear Rice Wines, called Michiu, made in Taiwan. Recommended Gluten free brands include: *Michiu Rice Wine, Taiwan Premium Cooking Michiu, Michiu by Qian Hu, Fortune Cookie Wine Michiu, Tai Jade Michiu, Cooking Spirits Michiu, Cooking Michiu.* If you can't find Rice Wine, Pale Dry Sherry or Mirin are both good substitutes.

Rice Wrapper/Rice Paper Wrapper – these are round or square thin sheets of brittle Rice Paper, usually made in Vietnam. They can be cut and fried to make puffy crackers or they can be rehydrated and used to wrap ingredients. We use them in this cookbook as a Gluten-Free Wrapper for Baked Spring Rolls.

Salt – this is an essential seasoning ingredient in all cooking, as it is one of the basic Five Flavors in Chinese cooking. It is used for enhancing the flavor of foods and as a preservative. We like to use *Maldon Sea Salt and Himalayan Pink Salt.*

Chinese Sausage/Lap Chong/Lap Cheong – a dried fatty Pork Sausage that has a unique sweet taste and is used in a number of Chinese dishes. Unfortunately, many Chinese Sausages contain Soy Sauce that is made with Wheat and/or MSG and/or Red Food Coloring. We found brands that were Gluten Free, but had food coloring and no MSG and another one that did not have food coloring, but did have MSG. So, we have given you a recipe for Chinese Bacon Bits, which is cured Pork Belly with the flavors of Chinese Sausage, minus the allergenic ingredients.

Toasted Sesame Oil – an oil made from toasted and pressed Sesame Seeds with a distinctive nutty flavor and smell. It is considered an essential ingredient in Chinese cuisine. It is used in many, if not most dishes and especially in salad dressings. Chinese Chefs will often use a few drops to finish a dish and give it a tantalizing aroma.

Sesame Seeds – the seeds from the Sesame plant. They are very small and can be black or white (actually a tan color) and both are used in Chinese Cooking. They have a light nutty flavor are often used as a garnish for salads, baked goods and candies.

Sesame Paste/Tahini – a paste made from ground Sesame Seeds that can be either Sweet or Savory. Chinese Sesame Paste is usually made from toasted Sesame Seeds. Tahini is a good alternative from many Middle Eastern countries. Each kind of Sesame Paste has a different consistency from very runny to very stiff. In Chinese cooking, Sesame Paste is usually made into a thin sauce and flavored with other condiments or sweetened and used in pastries.

Shallot – a member of the Allium family that is closely related to Onions. Shallots have a red papery skin and tend to have two large cloves. Smaller than most Onions, they also have a more elongated shape. They also have a milder flavor than Onions and a higher water content and melt into sauces better. The Chinese particularly like to fry Shallots to use as a garnish and then cook other dishes with the remaining flavored Oil.

Pale Dry Sherry – this is a good substitute for Rice Wine in Chinese cooking.

Shitake Mushroom/Winter Mushroom – *see* Mushrooms

Sichuan Peppercorns – these are the small dried fruits of the Prickly Ash Tree. They have a numbing effect on the lips and tongue and are a main ingredient in the Ma La flavor profile of Sichuan cooking. They are sometimes used whole in Spiced Broths, but they are usually ground with Salt to make a Seasoning blend and are considered an essential ingredient in Sichuan Chili Oil.

Sorghum – an ancient grain of China that was used as a cereal, made into liquor called Baiju and ground into a flour to make flatbread. Sorghum is naturally Gluten Free and often used as an ingredient in Gluten Free Flour mixes.

Soybeans – a legume that has been one of the most important foods in China for centuries. Soybeans are high in protein and are a good meat substitute. Soybeans can be made into many other products such as Soy Sauce, Tamari, Soy Milk, Tofu, Tofu Skins, Soy Bean Pastes, Fermented Black Beans, Soy Flour and Soybean Oil. These are all made from reconstituted dried Soybeans. Soybeans can also be fried and eaten as a snack or used as a garnish. Immature Soybeans, usually called Edamame are sold frozen and need to be boiled. They can also be eaten as a snack or used as an ingredient in a variety of other dishes.

Soy Sauce/Tamari – a condiment made from fermented Soybeans that is black and has varying amounts of saltiness. It is considered an essential ingredient in Chinese cooking. Unfortunately, most commercial brands usually contain wheat. *Recommended Gluten Free Soy Sauce brands include: Kikkoman; Joyce Chen; Fruit Island; Lee Kum Kee; Kari-Out; Little Soya; and Wa Ja Shan (both regular and low sodium). Korean Soy Sauce is always Gluten Free.*

Tamari is basically the same product but is often a little thicker and a little less salty. Most are also Gluten Free but be sure to check the label. *Gluten Free brands include: San-J, Eden, Ohsawa, Simply Balanced and Yamasa.*

We used San-J Tamari, both regular and low sodium along with Kikkoman Gluten Free Soy Sauce to make the recipes in this cookbook.

If you are trying to avoid soy-based sauces, Coconut Aminos is a good option. However, it is lighter in color and flavor and is also a little bit sweeter. We recommend *Coconut Secret's Coconut Amino Sauce.*

Sweet Soy Sauce/Kecap Manis – this is a sweetened version of Soy Sauce from Indonesia that has become popular in Chinese cooking. It is made by cooking Soy Sauce with Sugar so that it becomes thick and caramelized. It is used as a drizzle on vegetables, as a dipping sauce by itself or as the base for other sauces. Unfortunately, almost all Sweet Soy Sauces we have found contain gluten, except *Kikkoman*, which is thinner than the traditional kind, but you can cook it down. We have included a homemade version in this cookbook.

Spinach – a dark green leafy vegetable from the Amaranth family with tender leaves. Spinach has high nutritional value and is a popular vegetable in Chinese cuisine. The Chinese usually cook Spinach and it is used as an ingredient in soups and is often sautéed.

Star Anise – a spice pod from an evergreen tree, similar in taste to aniseed, licorice or fennel with a distinctive star-like shape. It is widely used in Chinese cooking to infuse flavor into soups and braised dishes. It is also an important ingredient in Five Spice Powder.

Sugar/Sucrose – a sweet soluble carbohydrate made from plants. It is used in preparing food to add a sweet taste and is especially important for pastries and desserts. People have a natural desire for sugar since it is one of the Five Basic Flavors. Chinese cooks will often use a bit of sugar in their savory dishes to bring out the flavor. Types used in this cookbook are *White Cane Sugar, Brown Cane Sugar, Powdered Sugar and especially Rock Candy Sugar, which gives many braised dishes a special sheen.*

Sweet Potato Starch – a powdery flour derived from Sweet Potatoes. It is used for breading Chicken in Taiwanese Popcorn Chicken and for making the Taiwanese Ba Wan Dumplings and Crystal Dumplings.

Tamari – Most are also Gluten Free, but be sure to check. Also *see* Soy Sauce

Tapioca Pearls – these are formed from starch extracted from the Cassava plant and formed into little balls. When these Tapioca Pearls are cooked in a liquid, they swell and become soft, chewy and translucent. They are most often used for puddings and when larger, are used in drinks.

Tapioca Starch – a powdery flour extracted from the Cassava/Yucca Root. It is a common ingredient in Gluten Free Baking Mixes as it adds a chewy texture. In this cookbook, it is a very important ingredient used in Dumpling Wrappers and flour blends used to make baked goods.

Tea/Cha – an aromatic beverage created by pouring boiling water over the cured leaves of the Camilla Senesis plant. Tea is one of the most popular drinks in the world, originating in China and tea drinking is a very important part of Chinese life. They drink it all day, during meals and for health. The Chinese believe that Tea is life enhancing and helps you digest fats. The most important teas from China are classified as: *White, Green, Oolong, Black and Post-fermented/Dark Tea,* all of which have very different flavors. Tea is sometimes flavored with other ingredients like Jasmine or Osmanthus flowers.

Chinese Herbal Teas – these are actually infusions or tisanes that in Chinese culture usually involve flowers, fruit, roots or herbs. These are steeped in boiling water and are often used medicinally. Some of the popular Chinese Herbal Teas are: *Chrysanthemum, Hibiscus, Ginseng, Goji Berry and Jujube.* Often several of these ingredients are combined.

Tofu/Doufu – this is a staple food in Chinese cooking. It is made from Soy Milk coagulated with either Gypsum or Nigari. Then the curds are pressed into blocks. The firmness of Tofu is based on how much water is pressed out of the blocks. As the firmness increases, so does protein and fat content. Tofu is usually white or off-white and has very little flavor. However, it does absorb the flavors of sauces and marinades very well. Tofu can easily be made to have different textures and is commonly used as a meat replacement, particularly in Chinese Vegetarian cooking. Types used in this cookbook include: Soft, Medium or Firm Tofu along with Tofu Skins, Tofu Skin Sticks and Egg Tofu. Tofu can be sautéed in stir-fry dishes, added to soups, baked, smoked and fried. It is an incredibly versatile ingredient.

Egg Tofu – this is a particular kind of Tofu made with Eggs and Soy Milk. It is pale yellow and does taste like Eggs. It is actually quite easy to make at home if you make your own Soymilk and is found in Asian markets sold in plastic tubes.

Tofu Skin/Bean Curd Sheets/Yuba – a thin sheet that is skimmed off the pot when making Soy Milk. It is sold both fresh or dried. It has a rubbery texture and can be used in a number of ways – fried, braised and as wrappers for a variety of fillings. Tofu Skin absorbs the flavor of the sauce it is cooked in or marinated in and it is used extensively as a meat substitute in Chinese Vegetarian cooking. When the sheets are rolled up and dried, they are called Bean Curd or Tofu Sticks.

Vanilla Extract – this flavoring ingredient is made from the pod of a special Orchid. It is called a Vanilla Bean and is soaked in ethanol to release its unique flavor. It is used to add a special flavor to many sweets and is considered an important ingredient in baked goods.

Vegetable Broth – a savory liquid made with water and various vegetables and aromatics like Garlic and Onions. Chinese cooking uses a lot of Chicken Broth and this is a Vegetarian and Vegan substitute. Commercially prepared Vegetable Broths are available in cans and cartons for ease of use. We offer a recipe for homemade Vegetable Broth that you can keep in your freezer until you need it.

Vinegar – an important condiment in Chinese cooking that adds a sour flavor. Chinese varieties are usually made from fermenting Rice. The most famous kind, Chinkiang Vinegar is made with Wheat, so look for clear Rice Vinegar or Japanese Brown Rice Vinegar. You can also find Rice Vinegar with some Sugar added and that is called Seasoned Rice Vinegar (to make it yourself – the ratio is: for each Tablespoon of Rice Vinegar, add one teaspoon of Sugar). Other Vinegars that can be used include: Coconut Vinegar, which is less sour than most or White Balsamic Vinegar, which is made from grapes and usually quite strong. Vinegar is used to make Pickles, Dipping Sauces, Salad Dressings and sweet and sour sauces.

Water Chestnuts – the corm of a plant that grows in marshes. There is a brown skin that must be peeled with a crisp, white flesh that tastes slightly sweet. Water Chestnuts can be used raw, but they are most often found canned and have the distinction of remaining crisp even when processed and cooked. They are used for a crunchy texture in many dishes.

Watercress – a leafy green plant that grows in the water with small leaves on narrow fibrous stems. It has a peppery bite since it is related to Mustard and Radishes and is also part of the Brassica family of plants. It is considered highly nutritious.

Worcestershire Sauce – a dark fermented liquid condiment, originally made in England. It is made with a combination of ingredients that usually include Tamarind and Molasses and is used to add a tangy, salty and Umami flavor to foods. The Chinese call is *Spicy Soy Sauce* and use it at Dim Sum restaurants as a dip for Meatballs and Egg Rolls. Recommended Gluten Free and Anchovy free choices include: *Wan Ja Shan*, *The Wizards Sauce*, *365 Everyday Value, and Edward and Sons.*

Xanthan Gum – a polysaccharide made from fermenting simple sugars. It is used in baking to replace the elasticity and stickiness of Gluten for making Gluten Free breads and pastries.

Yeast – a leavening agent used to give loft to breads and cakes. Active Dry Yeast and Rapid Rise Yeast are the kinds we used in this cookbook.

Yu Choi/Yu Choy/Edible Rape – a green leafy vegetable with a medium length stalk, dark green leaves and small yellow flowers. It is a member of the Brassica family and is related to Bok Choy. The Chinese call it *Oil Vegetable* since the seeds are used to make cooking oil.

Zucchini/Courgette/Marrow/Summer Squash – the long, thin skinned green fruit of the Summer Squash family native to the Americas. It is usually used at a fairly early stage of development when the Zucchini is up to 6 inches long when the seeds are still soft and immature. It can be eaten raw or cooked in a variety of ways, which makes the flesh very soft. It has a mild flavor and works well with stronger flavors.

CHAPTER 3

Chinese Cooking Primer

Preparation is the key to good Chinese cooking. The trick is to have everything cut ahead of time and ready to be cooked. Then the actual cooking time is usually quite fast, except when you are braising or making soup. One of the other tricks to Chinese cooking is to cut everything in the same dish to approximately the same size. That ensures that things cook evenly or you can cook foods in order of how long they take, remove them to add the next ingredient and add them all back together again. The similar size makes the dish easier to eat with chopsticks and is more visually appealing.

It has been said that you need very few pieces of kitchen equipment to make a good Chinese meal. In the past and even during the Cultural Revolution most Chinese kitchens only had about 8 pieces of equipment – a wok with a lid, a bamboo steamer tray, a stockpot, a spatula, a ladle, a wire mesh strainer, a cutting board and a very sharp knife. Of course, most of us have much more than that!

Essential Equipment

Knife/Knives – We recommended that you have a at least one good Chef's knife that you keep very sharp. If you like, you can also find good uses for a Paring knife, a Santoku Knife to slice vegetables, and/or a Cleaver to cut meat, pound meat and smash garlic.

Cutting Boards – These can be made of wood, plastic or other composite materials and come in various sizes. Wood Cutting Boards are more traditional and help keep knives sharp, although we advise that you keep separate cutting boards for meat and vegetables.

Ladle – This is a utensil with a round, cup-sized holder at the bottom for serving soups and sauces.

Soup Pot – This is a large pot used for making broth or soup or to cook a whole chicken.

Steamer Pot or Bamboo Steamer Basket placed in a wok – These are used for steaming foods on a flat surface, usually lined with cabbage leaves and need to be large enough to contain a plate or a bowl.

Wire Mesh Strainer – This is often called a Spider and is used to scoop food out of oil and to drain those foods of oil, or to clean out the crumbs in the bottom of a fryer.

Wok, Spatula and Lid – This is a cooking pot, preferably made of Carbon Steel. The traditional wok is rounded on the bottom and used on top of a Wok Holder over a gas flame or fire. Flat-bottomed woks are designed for electric stoves and have a long handle. A special wok spatula, usually made of metal, helps toss the food while scraping the sides of the wok. The lid is used for covering the wok when using it for steaming. It is important to season the wok before and after using and it is cleaned with very hot water with a stiff brush.

Other Pots and Pans

Baking Pans/Sheet Pans – These are metal pans made of steel or aluminum used in the oven or broiler to bake, roast or broil foods. They are also useful as trays lined with wax paper when making dumplings or to gather ingredients used in a dish. They come in ½ sheet (jellyroll) size along with ¼ sheet and ⅛ sheet size.

Braising Pot/Dutch Oven – This is a heavy enameled iron pot used for cooking foods for a long time in a relatively small amount of liquid and at low temperatures.

Cake Pans – These can be round or square and are used for baking and steaming cakes.

Clay Pot – This is a pot made of clay that can be used for braising stews or cooking rice on the stove and also for making soups. They can also be used for serving. However, they must be hand washed.

Non-stick Frying Pans with Lids – These are considered best for cooking dumplings or any egg dishes as they keep food from sticking to the pan.

Roasting Pan with Rack – This is used for cooking large pieces of meat in the oven for a long period of time. The rack keeps the meat from touching the liquid that accumulates.

Saucepans of various sizes – These are used for making sauces, boiling noodles, etc.

Other Useful Equipment

Bamboo Skewers - These are thin slivers of Bamboo wood with a pointed tip used to grill or broil meat. They can also be found in stainless steel, although Bamboo Skewers are much more authentic.

Chopsticks (long) – These are used to test oil (it bubbles when the chopstick is inserted, which means it is ready), used to stir eggs and to pluck food out of oil. They can also be placed 2 across in each direction in a wok to hold a plate for steaming.

Colander – This is a plastic or metal bowl with holes of varying sizes in it used to wash vegetables or rice.

Cookie or Biscuit Cutters – For Chinese food, use 3, 4 or 5-inch round and square Cookie or Biscuit Cutters used to cut dough to make Chinese dumplings and pastries.

Electric Deep Fryer – This is an electric appliance that keeps oil at a constant temperature for deep-frying. However, It is traditional in China to deep-fry in your wok.

Electric Rice Cooker – These electric appliance can be set to cook various types of rice and keeps the rice warm for hours.

Grater – There a number of different kinds of Graters now, usually made of Metal and they are used for shredding garlic, ginger and vegetables. We especially like the microplane graters.

Lettuce Knife – This is a special knife made of plastic used to cut Lettuce. It is designed to help prevent browning of the leaves.

Mandoline – This is a handheld utensil with blades of varying thickness used for slicing food into equally thick or thin slices. It comes with a food holder to protect your fingers from getting cut. It is especially helpful when making Vegetable Chips.

Mesh Gloves – These gloves are used to prevent cuts on the hand. These are particularly useful when grating food or using a Mandoline.

Meat Pounder – This is a mallet for food, usually made of metal or wood that makes cuts of meat thinner and more tender.

Mixing Bowls – These can be found of various sizes and are made of Metal, Glass or Plastic. They are used for holding ingredients until cooking with them or for mixing foods together, particularly Dumpling and Pastry Doughs.

Negi Cutter – This is a small Japanese knife with multiple blades that cuts Green Onions into shreds so that they will curl for garnish.

Oil Dispenser – This is a bottle with a special spout that allows the oil to drizzle out. It is very useful for pouring in the oil onto the sides of the wok. Smaller ones work well for dispensing Tamari or Sesame Oil.

Pressure Cooker – These can be used on a stovetop or they also can be found in electric models that allow programming.. They cook food quickly under pressure, which cooks food faster. They are especially good for braising large pieces of meat, stews or to cook dried soybeans or other beans.

Rice Bowls – These are small, heat-proof round bowls used for steaming small amounts of food or for serving rice.

Rolling Pins – These are usually made of wood or marble with side handles used for making dumpling wrappers and pastry dough. Chinese Rolling Pins are much smaller than the traditional Western ones and are usually about 5 inches long by about 1½ inches around and can be made from cutting off pieces of a dowel and sanding the ends.

Scissors/Kitchen Shears – These are very useful for snipping herbs, cutting Rice Paper Wrappers, Tofu Skins and for cutting through Chicken bones.

Sizzling Platters – These platters are made of metal and are heated in the oven, placed on a wooden serving tray and delivered to the table with the food spooned onto the hot platter so that it sizzles.

Spatulas – These are made of either metal or plastic and come in various widths. They are used to turn food over in frying pans or on baking sheets.

Steamer Liners – These are made either from parchment-like paper with holes or silicone mesh with holes. They keep dumplings and other steamed foods from sticking in the steamer.

Thermometers – used for testing the doneness of meats, assessing the temperature of frying oil and recognizing the stage in candy making.

Tofu Press – a small plastic box with rubber bands or two plates used with weights to release the water in tofu to give it a firmer texture.

Tongs – These are v-shaped implements used to pick up individual pieces of food. They are usually made of metal and sometimes have silicone tips and are very useful for turning food, as well as retrieving individual pieces of food from a pot.

Tortilla Press – This is a metal press used to flatten a piece of dough into a flat round shape. They come from Mexico and can be useful for making Dumpling Dough.

Vegetable Peelers – Although peeling can be done with a sharp knife, a sharp vegetable peeler makes peeling vegetables much easier. There is also a Julienne Peeler that makes quick work out of shredding hard vegetables like carrots and radishes.

Wire Strainer – This is a half-moon shaped wire rack that attaches to the side of the wok where fried food can be placed to drain off the excess oil.

Wok Brush – This is usually made of Bamboo and is used to clean a wok and removed stuck bits of food without the use of soap.

Wooden Spoons – These come in a variety of sizes and are used to stir food while braising with the benefit of not scratching the lining of the pot.

Cutting Methods

The Chinese are masters of the blade and they take the cutting of vegetables and meats very seriously. They believe that the size and therefore the texture of the ingredients influence the taste. One of the important rules in Chinese cutting techniques is to cut all of the ingredients in a dish the same size, except for garnishes. This ensures an even cooking time as well.

Chiffonade – This involves rolling greens or herbs and cutting them into thin strips.

Chop – This means to cut foods to about the size of a pea.

Crush – This involves smashing foods with the heavy, flat side of cleaver or the flat side of a Chef's Knife.

Diagonal Cutting – This is when you cut foods at a 45° angle, often used for vegetables and for green onions.

Dice – This means to cut foods into about a ½-inch square.

Cube – Cutting foods into about a 1-inch square.

Julienne – To cut food into matchstick size pieces about 1 – 1½-inches long by ¼-inch wide.

Mince – This means to cut food very fine (about the size of a grain of rice) and with meat, it almost creates a paste.

Pound – This involves hitting meat with a blunt end of the cleaver or a meat pounder to make the meat into thinner pieces.

Rolling Cut – To create this cut, you must turn vegetables, like carrots, and cut at a 45 degree angle after each quarter turn.

Sliver – This means to cut food into thin pieces about half the width of julienned pieces.

Shred – This breaks down vegetables into smaller and softer pieces. Use a fine shredder for foods like ginger and garlic and a wider shredder for other vegetables.

Slice – This involves cutting food into pieces about 1 to 1½-inch long and ¼-inch wide.

Straight Cutting – This means to cut foods straight down into slices.

Cooking Methods

Bake – Cooking food slowly in the dry heat of an oven. It is an important cooking method for pastries.

Broil – This is a setting on the oven that most closely mimics using a Barbecue. It is usually set at 500°F and helps food cook very rapidly.

Blanch – This involves precooking food, usually vegetables, by putting them in boiling water for just a few minutes.

Boiling – This means to cook food in very hot water or broth.

Braising or Red Cooking – This is a method of cooking meat or tofu in a relatively small amount of liquid and seasonings, at a simmer until the meat or tofu is very tender and full of flavor. The sauce becomes thick and rich and can be served with the food or used as a Master Sauce for future use.

Cold Mix – This is when you take blanched or precooked ingredients that are then combined together and refrigerated, allowing their flavors to blend.

Deep Frying – This is the method of cooking foods by immersing them in hot oil until they are crispy. The oil must be very hot in order to seal in the juices and prevent greasiness.

Dressing – This is the creation of a mixture of an acid combined with an oil and various seasonings to create a sauce for vegetables, as in a salad.

Dry Frying – This involves scorching food, either meat or vegetables, in a very hot wok without a sauce to achieve a dry texture.

Dry Roast – This means to cook ingredients in a pan or the oven with no oil, like seeds, until they are hot and lightly browned.

Dry Marinating – This is a mixture consisting of a combination of Salt, Sugar and Spices to create a rub for meat that flavors it before roasting or grilling.

Flash Frying – This involves cooking meat marinated in a sauce to which cornstarch or egg white has been added. The meat is drained from the marinade and added to a super, hot pan coated with heated oil and cooked quickly to seal in the juices.

Grilling – This means to cook food quickly and directly over hot charcoal or wood, which often chars the ingredients on the edges and makes food taste a bit smoky. Grill marks are considered desirable.

Hotpot – This is like a fondue of savory broth where each person cooks their own food and mixes up sauces to dip the food into before eating.

Jellying – Making foods that set into a jelly-like form when chilled in the refrigerator using gelatin or Agar Agar as the thickener. This technique is used for sweet desserts and for making the Chinese version of Aspic – jellied meat stock for Soup Dumplings.

Marinating – Creating a sauce mixture using herbs, spices, other condiments and usually an acid. The marinade may include other flavoring ingredients, such as scallions, onions, ginger, hot chilies, etc. The meat or tofu is soaked in the marinade for several hours up to 24 hours ahead to infuse it with flavors before cooking it.

Oil Blanching – This involves partially cook meat in hot oil – previously marinated in a mixture of cornstarch, egg white and rice wine – before adding to a dish so that the texture of the meat is tender, soft and smooth in texture.

Pan Frying – Cooking food in a frying pan with a small amount of oil to brown the foods on each side

Pickling – This involves placing food, usually vegetables, in an acidic and/or salty brining solution to preserve it for later use.

Poaching – This means to gently cook food, like Chicken, in a small amount of simmering water or broth to keep it tender.

Reducing Sauce – This is the result of cooking down the remaining sauce in a dish over a high heat until it reaches approximately half of its previous volume.

Roasting – This involves cooking food in the oven with dry heat. The outside of the food usually develops a crust, if cooking meat or caramelizes if cooking vegetables or tofu.

Salt Bake – This involves wrapping food, usually meat, in a thick layer of salt and then cooking in the hardened salt shell in the oven or on the grill

Scrambling – This means you take a soft ingredient, like eggs or tofu and cook it, stirring often until it forms small curds.

Simmering – This involves cooking a liquid on a low heat. This technique is particularly useful for soups, stews and braises.

Smoking – This means to cook food in direct contact with smoke so that it absorbs the smoke flavor and fragrance. In Chinese cooking, the usual source of the smoke is tea leaves.

Soaking – This is when you place dried vegetables, like Shitake Mushrooms, into water to rehydrate them.

Steaming – This is cooking food over boiling water on a rack over a steamer pot or in a bamboo steamer tray over a wok. Steaming preserves the flavor of the ingredients. Some foods are wrapped before steaming. This is also a method for cooking rice in a covered pot after most of the water had boiled down.

Steam Frying – This is when you cook food in a wok or frying pan with a small amount of oil as in Pan-Frying or Stir-Frying, and then adding a small amount of broth, water or other liquid to continue the cooking or completing the cooking process, as in dumplings. This technique is also used to soften the food as in sautéed greens or to impart a deeper flavor.

Stir Frying – This is the method of cooking food in a preheated hot wok that is then coated with a small amount of oil before the food to be cooked is added. The ingredients of a dish are precut about the same size and in relatively small pieces so that they cook quickly. The first ingredients are usually the aromatics -garlic, ginger, green onions, shallots or onions – and they are cooked until their aroma is released. Next the main ingredients, usually meat or tofu, is added, or the food is added in the order of how long it takes to cook each ingredient. Cooked ingredients may be removed to a plate until the other ingredients are done. Meat is usually cooked until just pink or opaque. The food is always cooked and tossed on high heat with a wok spatula. Then all of the ingredients are added back in and the dish is sauced and seasoned. Cooking time is fast so all ingredients must be prepped ahead of time.

Velveting – Meat that has been marinated in a mixture of cornstarch, rice wine and egg white is cooked briefly in boiling water or broth with oil added in before being added back into a stir-fry dish. It creates a soft and velvety texture.

Wine Steeping – This involves marinating cooked food, like chicken in Rice Wine before serving.

CHAPTER 4

Essential Chinese Recipes

This is the classic Chinese Chicken Broth made with Rice Wine, Ginger, Garlic and Green Onions. It is considered an essential ingredient in the Chinese kitchen. My grandfather almost always had a pot of this Broth simmering on his stove, but he usually used Chicken bones that he collected from deboning Chicken for other dishes. I usually double this recipe and keep some in both the refrigerator and freezer since it is used in so many dishes. If you don't have the time to make homemade Chicken Broth, use a high-quality low Sodium canned Chicken Broth and simmer with the seasonings for 30 minutes to create the Chinese flavor.

Chinese Chicken Broth

6 Chicken Drumsticks or Thighs or a combination,
or 4–5 Chicken Backs

10 cups Water

a 2-inch piece of Ginger, peeled and cut into slices

4 Green Onions, roots cut off and cut in half

2 Garlic cloves, peeled and smashed

½ cup Rice Wine

2 teaspoons Salt

Place Chicken pieces in a large pot and add Water, Green Onions, Ginger, Garlic cloves, Salt and Rice Wine. Bring to a boil and reduce heat to a simmer. Skim off foam. Cook for 1 hour and 15 minutes. Remove Chicken pieces from the soup. Strain the broth and cool, then refrigerate or freeze for future use. Pull the meat off the bones and save for another use.

Poached Chicken is needed in many recipes and here are two ways to do it using Chinese Chicken Broth. The Stovetop version is the classic recipe and makes good Shredded Chicken. The Oven Poached version is a relatively new technique where the Chicken is very tender and moist and is especially good when sliced and drizzled with sauces. Chicken has such mild flavor that it is the preferred meat for Chinese Salads.

Chinese Stovetop Poached Chicken

2 Bone-in Chicken Breast halves
4 cups Chinese Chicken Broth (see recipe)

Bring the Chicken Broth to a boil and add in the Chicken Breasts. Return broth to a boil and reduce heat to a simmer. Cook for 15 minutes and then turn off the stove and cover the pot with a lid. Let cool.

Pull the Chicken meat off the bones and pull apart with your fingers or two forks to create shreds.

Chinese Oven Poached Chicken

2 boneless, skinless Chicken Breast halves
4 cups Chinese Chicken Broth

Heat the oven to 300°F. Place Chicken Breasts into an ovenproof baking dish. Bring the Chicken Broth to a boil in a small pot and pour carefully over the Chicken Breasts. Place in the oven and cook for 1 hour or until a meat thermometer reads 155°F.

Remove from the oven and let cool. Cut into slices or shred.

This is the Vegetarian/Vegan replacement for Chinese Chicken Broth that is needed in so many dishes and it's delicious in its own right. The vegetables are not meant to be eaten after you've made the broth, as they have given up all of their flavor. Be sure to keep the peels on the vegetables to infuse this broth with more healthy nutrients!

Chinese Vegetable Broth

1 large Onion, trimmed, peeled and roughly chopped

1 Leek, ends trimmed, cut in half and sliced into 2-inch sections, then washed

4 Green Onions

2–3 Carrots, stem ends removed and roughly chopped (do not peel)

2 cups of Daikon Radish, washed and cut into chunks (do not peel)

2 stalks of Celery, trimmed and cut into small pieces

5 cups of Napa Cabbage stems (save leaves for another use)

10 cups Water

1½ Tablespoons Sea Salt

In a large soup pot, add in the Onion, Leeks, Carrots, Daikon Radish, Napa Cabbage Stems and Celery. Add in the Water and Salt and bring to a boil. Reduce heat to a simmer and cook for one hour. Strain to get a clear broth.

Dried Mandarin Orange Peel is a classical Chinese seasoning used primarily for Beef dishes. You can buy it already dried in most Asian grocery stores but it's quite easy to make at home. We dry it in the oven instead of in the sun as we live in Seattle. We use Mandarin Orange Peel for the traditional version of Steamed Beef Meatballs.

Dried Mandarin Orange Peel

Peel of two Mandarin Oranges

Heat the oven to 250°F. Take the Peel and scrape off the white pith with a small, serrated knife. Then cut into pieces. Place the Mandarin Orange Peel on a baking sheet. Place in the oven and turn the heat off. Remove the Mandarin Orange Peels when the oven is cool. Store in a glass jar until ready to use.

I used to buy Sichuan Chili Oil at the Asian Market, but it never tasted fresh enough and it is a much-needed ingredient in Chinese cooking. So, Stephen started making it at home. This recipe is very simple: just heat up some neutral flavored Oil and add in some Green Onions, Ginger and Sichuan Peppercorns with Sichuan Red Chili Flakes or sliced Red Chili Pods. The Chili Flakes will make it very red, while the sliced Chili Pods will make it look more orange. You let the mixture sit and steep overnight or longer, then strain it and use as desired. That's all it takes to make delicious Sichuan Chili Oil that can be used in so many ways!

Sichuan Chili Oil

1 cup Vegetable Oil

2 Green Onions, trimmed and cut into 3-inch pieces

a 2-inch piece of Ginger, peeled and smashed

¼ cup Sichuan Red Chili Flakes or 8 small dried Chili Pods, sliced

1 Tablespoon Sichuan Peppercorns, ground

½ teaspoon Salt

1 Star Anise pod

In a small frying pan, heat the Oil on medium heat. Add in the Green Onion, Ginger, Chili Flakes or Pods, Salt, Star Anise and Sichuan Peppercorns. Cook, stirring frequently until the Green Onions start to brown, being careful not to burn the chili flakes. Pour into a bowl. When cool, pour into a jar. Seal and let sit overnight in the refrigerator or longer. Then, strain and reseal to use for up to several months.

I went to a Dim Sum restaurant in Singapore a few years ago where I tasted a Chili Oil that was full of Chili Flakes and also bits of Garlic. I came home and asked Stephen if he would recreate it. He ended up using the Red Chili flakes that you usually use as a Pizza Topping, since they are easy to find. He also used lots of Garlic and Shallot bits, which became crispy when cooked slowly. This is now my favorite Chili Oil, as it is can be spooned over so many foods. We usually make a big batch as it goes so quickly. It also makes a wonderful gift.

Stephen's Crispy Chili Oil

1 cup Vegetable Oil
8 Garlic cloves, minced
½ cup Shallots, minced
2 Tablespoons – ¼ cup
Red Chili Flakes

½ teaspoon Salt
½ teaspoon Sugar
a pinch of Five Spice Powder

Put the Oil in the frying pan and add the Garlic and Shallots. Bring to a simmer on low heat and cook until they are light golden brown. Remove the browned bits to a plate with a mesh spider. Then add in the Red Chili Flakes, the Salt, Sugar and Five Spice Powder. Bring the Chili Oil back to a simmer on low heat and cook, stirring often until the Chili Flakes sound crisp when you stir them. Then add in the reserved Garlic and Shallots. Remove from heat and let cool. Place in a jar and refrigerate until ready to use.

There are three basic Chinese Seasoned Salts: Chili Salt, Five Spice Salt and Sichuan Peppercorn Salt. They can all be used for seasoning or to enhance any dish where Salt is required. The Five Spice Salt makes a great rub when added to Sugar and in Hawaii, it is often served on the table. Both the Five Spice Salt and the Sichuan Peppercorn Salt are also wonderful when sprinkled on fried foods.

Chinese Seasoned Salts

CHILI SALT

¼ cup fine Sea Salt
2 Tablespoons Chili Flakes
¼ teaspoon of Sugar

Crush the Chili Flakes in a mortar with the pestle and add in Salt and Sugar. Combine and store in an airtight jar.

FIVE SPICE SALT

¼ cup fine Sea Salt
1 teaspoon Five Spice Powder
¼ teaspoon of Sugar

Mix together and use as a dip, sprinkle on many foods or add some sugar to make a rub. Store in an airtight jar.

SICHUAN PEPPER SALT

¼ cup fine Sea Salt
2 Tablespoons Sichuan Peppercorns
¼ teaspoon of Sugar

Brown peppercorns and salt in a dry frying pan until it smells fragrant. Remove and put into a mortar and pestle. Crush until the Peppercorns are in small pieces. Store in an airtight jar.

Oyster Sauce is a staple in the Chinese Pantry, but it's often off-limits for those with food allergies and intolerances. Although there are now Vegan Oyster Sauces available to buy, most of them are made with Wheat. Well, here's an alternative. This recipe uses the savory flavor of dried Shitake Mushrooms to increase the Umami flavor of the Tamari. If you don't want to make the powdered Mushrooms yourself, you can buy this ingredient online. I think Mushroom Tamari is absolutely delicious used with steamed and stir-fried vegetables and it's an important ingredient in Char Siu Bao filling.

Mushroom Tamari - Vegan Oyster Sauce

1 cup Low Sodium Tamari or GF Soy Sauce

1 cup Water

4–6 dried Shitake Mushrooms or
about ¾ cup of Shitake Mushroom Powder

2 Tablespoons Sugar

Grind the Shitake Mushrooms in a spice grinder until they become powdered.

In a small saucepan, heat the Tamari, Sugar, Mushroom Powder and Water. Whisk to combine. Bring to a boil over medium heat. Then reduce heat and simmer for 10 minutes. Cool and then pour into a bottle and refrigerator for several days before using. It will keep in the refrigerator for months. Strain if desired.

This is a pantry staple in Chinese Cuisine. It is actually a popular condiment all over Asia and is called Sweet Soy Sauce. In Indonesia, it is called Kecap Manis. We make it and keep it in the refrigerator to use whenever we need it and it stays good for a long time due to the high sugar content. Use it as a drizzle sauce for any bitter green vegetables and as an ingredient in other sauces that need more sweetness.

Sweet Tamari Sauce

1 cup Low Sodium Tamari or GF Soy Sauce
½ cup Brown Sugar
3 Tablespoons Water

Put mixture in a small frying pan. Bring to a boil and then reduce heat to a simmer. Cook for about 10–15 minutes or until the mixture coats the back of a spoon or leaves an open streak in the pan when you mix it. Cool and pour into a squeeze bottle container. Sweet Tamari will keep for months in the refrigerator.

Chinese Bacon and Sausage are important ingredients for many dishes, but they almost always contain Soy Sauce and Rice Wine made with Wheat and often contain MSG and Red Dye too. So, we created a homemade version of Chinese Bacon with the flavors of Chinese Sausage that takes just a few days of curing in the refrigerator before it is ready to use.

Chinese Bacon Bits

8 ounces of Pork Belly, cut into a small dice
½ teaspoon Sugar
½ teaspoon Five Spice Salt
1 teaspoon Tamari or GF Soy Sauce
1 teaspoon Rice Wine

Mix together all the ingredients in a bowl and place in the refrigerator, uncovered, so that it will dry out a bit. Leave for at least one day up to three days to cure before using.

When ready to use, place Bacon in a frying pan and cook until the fat is rendered. Use as desired as a garnish or in dishes like Savory Radish Cake and Sticky Rice in Lotus Leaves.

This was my favorite garnish as a child and I could eat handfuls of these crisp noodles whenever my Mother made them. I loved the crunch and the fact that they also dissolve in your mouth. Nowadays, I most often use these for my Mom's Chinese Chicken Salad and for any other Salad that would benefit from their light crunchiness. I usually serve them on the side for people to add themselves, as they soften quickly when they touch the dressing.

Fried Glass Noodles

1 package Glass Noodles (Mung Bean/Sai Fun), about 6–8 ounces
4 cups of Oil

Place Oil in a wok or deep fryer. Place the Noodles into a large, sealing Plastic Bag. Crush the noodles lightly with your hands to break them up or use Kitchen Scissors to cut into a desired length.

Line a plate or baking pan with paper towels. When the Oil is hot (375°F), add in about ½ cup of Noodles at a time. They will puff up dramatically very fast and become white. Remove immediately with a spider and place on the paper towels to drain. Repeat until all Noodles are cooked. Use as a garnish or place into the same storage bag at room temperature until you are ready to use them. You can reuse the Oil for other fried foods.

Frying Tofu Skins results in a delightfully crunchy snack or garnish very similar in taste and texture to fried Wonton Wrappers, without the gluten. Fried Tofu Skins don't have much flavor on their own, so we sprinkle them with the Chinese Seasoned Salt of your choice. We use Fried Tofu Skins primarily as a garnish for salads although you can eat them like chips too.

Fried Tofu Skin Threads

3 sheets of dried Tofu Skins
3–4 cups Vegetable Oil
Chinese Seasoned Salt

Cut the Tofu Skins into thin strips with kitchen shears. Heat the Oil in a wok or deep fryer to 375°F. Drop in a small handful of Tofu Threads. Fry until crisp and browned. Remove from the Oil with a spider. Drain on a paper towel covered plate. Repeat until all the Tofu Skin Threads are cooked. Sprinkle with the Chinese Seasoned Salt of your choice.

CHAPTER 5

Dips, Relishes & Sauces

Chili Garlic Sauce is an essential pantry staple if you are making any dishes that are spicy. Of course, you can buy this sauce in an Asian Market and there are some good ones, but many of them contain MSG and most are too hot for me. Stephen created a Chili Garlic Sauce that has a wonderful fresh flavor and you can add in some Red Bell Pepper to tone down the heat if you want it to be milder.

Chili Garlic Sauce

4 Red Jalapeños stemmed, seeded and chopped
½ of a small Red Pepper
4 cloves Garlic, chopped
½ teaspoon Salt
1 ½ tablespoons Sugar
1 ½ tablespoons Rice Vinegar

Put all the ingredients in a food processor or blender. Process only until the mixture reaches a coarse texture. Taste and adjust, adding extra salt or sugar, if desired and add in the Red Bell Pepper if it is too hot. Puree until smooth. Transfer the mixture to a small saucepan and bring to a boil over medium heat. Then lower the heat and simmer for about 5 minutes. Remove the sauce from the heat and set aside to cool. Transfer to a jar and store in the refrigerator.

This is a wonderful Sweet and Sour Dipping Sauce based on the Chili Garlic Sauce above, but you can also use a jarred Chili Garlic Sauce instead. We like this sauce best tossed with Fried Chicken or Tofu and it's one of our favorite dips for Egg Rolls.

Sweet Chili Garlic Dipping Sauce

¼ cup Chili Garlic Sauce
½ cup Water
2 ½ Tablespoons Rice Vinegar
2 Tablespoons Sugar
¼ teaspoon Salt
1 tablespoon Cornstarch

Combine all ingredients in a small saucepan, cook on low heat until the sauce thickens. Transfer to a bowl and use as a dip or toss with Fried Chicken or Fried Tofu.

This is the Dumpling Sauce that I grew up with, and we all still love it. Since we ate Dumplings weekly, I watched my Grandfather make this sauce so many times and I can still see him pouring it into little bowls - he never measured. The trick I learned from him is that you first pour the Rice Vinegar in the bowl and then add the Soy Sauce in until the mixture is almost the same color as the Soy Sauce by itself, just a little clearer.

We use Tamari or Gluten Free Soy Sauce now and add in some Sugar, Green Onions and/or Ginger. I like to put in just the Green Onions, both my sons must also add in the Ginger and they, along with my daughters-in-law love it with the Chili Oil added in too. Any way you make it, dumplings taste better with Dumpling Sauce!

Lowe Family Dumpling Sauce

¼ cup Tamari or GF Soy Sauce
¼ cup Rice Vinegar
½–1 Tablespoon Sugar
1 teaspoon finely sliced
Green Onions

OPTIONAL
A few slivers of fresh peeled Ginger
½–1 Tablespoon of Chili Oil

Mix Tamari, Rice Vinegar and Sugar together in a small bowl. Add in the
Chili Oil, if using. Sprinkle with Green Onion pieces and/or Ginger and let
the mixture sit for about 15 minutes before serving. It keeps for several days
in the refrigerator.

This is a classic Dumpling Sauce used everywhere in the Sichuan Province, mostly
used for dressing boiled Wontons. You can adjust the amount of Chili Oil to taste. We
especially love this sauce poured over a big bowl of Boiled Dumplings.

Sichuan Dumpling Sauce

3–4 Tablespoons Sichuan Chili Oil
or Stephen's Crispy Chili Oil

1 Tablespoon toasted Sesame Oil

2 Tablespoons Rice Vinegar

2 Tablespoons Tamari
or GF Soy Sauce

1 Tablespoon Sugar

2 Garlic cloves minced

2 Green Onions finely sliced

1 Tablespoon toasted
Sesame Seeds

OPTIONAL
½ teaspoon Sichuan Pepper Salt

In a small bowl, add in the Sichuan Chili Oil, Sesame Oil, Tamari and Sugar,
Garlic and Green Onions. Stir and add in the Sesame Seeds and the Sichuan
Peppercorns or Peppercorn Salt, if using. Refrigerate until ready to use.

We like to serve Vegetable Dumplings and Egg Rolls with a Sweet Tamari Dipping Sauce that is flavored with Garlic and White Pepper. If you would like to make it hotter, add in some Chili Garlic Sauce to liven it up.

Sweet Tamari Garlic Dumpling Sauce

4 cloves Garlic minced
¼ cup Sweet Tamari
2 Tablespoons Rice Vinegar
¼ teaspoon White Pepper

2 teaspoons Vegetable Oil
OPTIONAL
¼ – ½ teaspoon Chili Garlic Sauce

Heat the Oil until hot. Add Garlic and stir until you smell the fragrance. Mix in the Sweet Tamari, Rice Vinegar, White Pepper and Chili Garlic Sauce (if using) and remove from heat. Serve immediately or refrigerate until ready to use.

My friend Sabine often makes Dumplings with me and this is her version of a Dumpling Sauce that was popular in Taiwan when she lived there. We adapted it slightly to use Rice Vinegar instead of Chinkiang Vinegar, which unfortunately contains wheat. So, we sweetened it slightly with Brown Sugar to mellow the sharpness of the Rice Vinegar. This sauce is delicious with any Dumplings!

Taiwanese Dumpling Sauce

¼ cup Tamari or GF Soy Sauce
2 Tablespoons Rice Vinegar
2 Garlic cloves minced

1 teaspoon toasted Sesame Oil
1 teaspoon Brown Sugar

Mix all ingredients together and let sit for at least 15 minutes to let the flavors meld. This sauce keeps in the refrigerator for several days.

General Tso's Chicken is one of the most popular dishes in America and while it is based on the classic flavor profile of Hunanese food, it was actually Chef Peng Chang-kuei who created this dish in Taiwan while catering for foreign dignitaries. He named it after a famous Hunan General from his hometown and it was a sour, hot and salty dish flavored with Garlic and Ginger. He eventually opened his own restaurant in New York, where he started adding a bit of Sugar to the dish. Several chefs in New York copied his dish and made it even sweeter for the American palate and changed what was a stir-fry dish into a fried chicken dish with a sweet and sour sauce.

Our version of this sauce substitutes Rice Vinegar for the traditional Chinkiang Black Vinegar, since it contains wheat. You can also make this sauce as hot as you like, as Hunan food is usually very hot. You can toss this sauce with Chinese Fried Chicken or Tofu, but you will need to double the recipe. We usually serve it as a dip on the side.

General Tso's Sauce

2 Tablespoons Vegetable Oil
2 large Garlic cloves minced
1 ½ Tablespoons grated Ginger
3–4 Scallions, white and light green parts only, cut into small pieces
1–2 teaspoons Red Chili Flakes or 4–6 whole Chilies de Arbol
¼ teaspoon White Pepper
⅓ cup Tamari or GF Soy Sauce

⅓ cup Chicken or Vegetable Broth
¼ cup Rice Vinegar
2 Tablespoons Rice Wine
¼ cup Sugar
1 teaspoon toasted Sesame Oil
2 teaspoons Cornstarch mixed with 2 Tablespoon Cold Water

In a small bowl, mix together the Tamari, Broth, Rice Vinegar, Rice Wine and the Sugar. Set aside.

Heat the Oil in a frying pan. Add in the Garlic, Ginger, Green Onions and Red Chili Flakes (or whole Chiles) and White Pepper. Cook until you can smell the fragrance. Add in the sauce mixture and cook until it comes to a boil. Stir in the Cornstarch slurry and cook until thickened. Finally add the Sesame Oil and stir to combine. Toss with Chinese Fried Chicken or Tofu or serve on the side as a dip.

Think of this sauce as a Chinese version of Chimichurri or Salsa Verde. You can make it as hot as you like and it is absolutely delicious with any kind of meat, used as a dip for fried foods or drizzled onto any of the Wraps and Sandwich Rolls.

Cilantro and Green Chili Relish

2 cups of Cilantro Leaves

2 cups of chopped Green Onions

1 1-inch chunk of Ginger, peeled and grated

1 or more Serrano Chiles, seeds and membrane removed, cut into small pieces

¼ cup toasted Sesame Oil

¼ cup Vegetable Oil

¼ cup Rice Vinegar

1–2 cloves of Garlic, minced

1 teaspoon Salt

½ teaspoon Sugar

Place all ingredients in a food processor or blender and puree. Serve immediately or refrigerate to serve later.

This is a classic sauce in China that became popularized in the U.S. by the Momofuku Restaurant, but it is actually made by Chinese home cooks everywhere. The proportions of ingredients can be altered to suit your taste. Stephen and I like it on the savory side, so we add more Tamari. My Mother preferred it to be a bit sweet and always added a pinch of sugar. This sauce is wonderful over any kind of roasted Meat or Tofu. It is also good drizzled over the Green Onion Pancake Wraps and Rou Jia Mo Sandwich Rolls.

Green Onion and Ginger Relish

4 Green Onions, about ½ cup,
trimmed and cut into very thin slices

1 Tablespoon grated Ginger

2 Tablespoons Tamari or GF Soy Sauce

1 teaspoon Rice Vinegar

1 ½ teaspoons Sugar

½ teaspoon toasted Sesame Oil

Mix all ingredients together and let sit for at least 15 minutes to let the flavors meld. It will hold in the refrigerator for up to 3 days.

This is one of those recipes that came about totally by accident. Many years ago, my kids and I were at a Dim Sum restaurant and my younger son ordered some French Fries and of course they were served with Ketchup. A plate of Steamed Meatballs was also on the table and Stephen doused them with Worcestershire Sauce like everyone else, but he didn't like the flavor so he added some of his brother's Ketchup. He loved the combination and this sauce was born. It's very similar to Japanese Katsu Sauce and we love it with all kinds of fried foods as well. These days, I like to add in a bit of Sugar and we often add a little bit of Chili Sauce to spice it up too.

Meatball Dipping Sauce

¼ cup Worcestershire Sauce

¼ cup Ketchup

OPTIONAL

1 teaspoon Sugar

1 or more teaspoons Chili Sauce or Sriracha

Mix the Worcestershire Sauce, Ketchup, Sugar and Chili Sauce together in a small bowl.

Why make Chinese Hot Mustard when you can buy it in a jar at the grocery store? Because you can personalize and make it hotter, mellower or sweeter when you make it at home. This is our recipe for Chinese Hot Mustard. We use it as a dipping sauce for Char Siu Pork or as a spread for Rou Jia Mo Sandwiches.

Chinese Hot Mustard

¼ cup ground Mustard Powder
1 teaspoon Sugar
¼ teaspoon Salt
¼ cup Cold Water
2 teaspoons Vegetable Oil

In a small bowl, combine the Mustard, Sugar and Salt. Stir in the Water and Oil and whisk until smooth. Refrigerate until ready to use.

Orange Chicken is a dish that was developed by Panda Express in Hawaii with Orange Juice as the major flavoring component of the sauce. It is based on the Hunan dish of Orange Chicken, which uses dried Orange Peel. We like to make this copycat sauce using fresh Mandarin Orange Juice, as it's a bit tangier although you can certainly substitute Orange Juice. This is a family favorite now and we use it as a dip for Fried Chicken or Tofu, although you can certainly toss it all together instead, but then be sure to serve it immediately.

Mandarin Orange Sauce

1 Tablespoon of Vegetable Oil

¼ cup of minced Shallot

1 Tablespoon Ginger, peeled and grated

1 Garlic clove minced

½ cup Mandarin Orange Juice (about 6 medium)

2 Tablespoons Rice Vinegar

2 Tablespoons Tamari or GF Soy Sauce

2 Tablespoons Sugar

⅓ cup Chicken Broth

1 Tablespoon of Cornstarch

In a small bowl, mix together the Mandarin Orange Juice, Rice Wine Vinegar, Tamari and Sugar. In another bowl, stir together the Chicken Broth and Cornstarch.

In a non-stick frying pan, heat the oil and add in the Shallot, Ginger and Garlic. Cook until you can smell the fragrance. Stir in the Orange Mixture and bring to a boil. Reduce heat and simmer for 5 minutes. Taste and add more Tamari or Vinegar if desired. Then, add in the Chicken Stock and Cornstarch and stir until thickened.

Serve as a Dipping Sauce or toss with Chinese Fried Chicken or Tofu.

Chinese Plum Sauce is traditionally served with Peking Duck, although it is also quite popular as a dipping sauce for fried food, like Eggrolls or Chinese Fried Chicken or Tofu. Plum Sauce is usually quite sweet so Stephen created a version of Plum Sauce that is more tart and savory. We make a lot in the summer, usually quadrupling this recipe and then keeping it in the freezer.

Chinese Plum Sauce

1 cup diced and peeled dark skinned Plums, packed tightly (about 2 large)

2 Tablespoons Water

½ Tablespoon Vegetable Oil

2 Tablespoons minced Shallots

1 Tablespoon Rice Vinegar

1 teaspoon Tamari or GF Soy Sauce

¼ teaspoon Salt

a pinch of Five Spice Powder

In a small frying pan, heat the Vegetable Oil and add the Shallots. Cook until the Shallots soften. Add the Plums and Water along with the Rice Vinegar, Tamari, Salt and Five-Spice Powder. Simmer on medium low heat for 5 minutes, stirring often. Mash the Plum Sauce with a potato masher. If you want a smoother sauce, you can puree it in a food processor or a blender. Taste and adjust by adding more Sugar if you like it sweeter.

Cool and serve or put into a small glass jar and refrigerate or freeze until ready to use.

This is the red Sweet and Sour Sauce invented in American Chinese restaurants. It was first introduced in the dish, Sweet and Sour Pork. In China, there are a number of sauces that are a bit sweet and a bit sour, combining the tastes of Sugar and Vinegar. But, this kind of Sweet and Sour Sauce differs in that it is much sweeter and usually contains Pineapple, Green Pepper and Ketchup. It has become an ubiquitous sauce used as an Egg Roll Dipping Sauce or for crispy Noodles. Although most people from China find it strange, it is delicious in its own way. It is especially good with fried foods of all kinds.

This recipe comes from my cousin Cary, who is also a great cook. About 15 years ago, I was having a Chinese New Year Party and made Pork Meatballs, but I forgot to make any dipping sauce. He whipped this up and it was such a hit! Of course, he gave us the recipe and we have been making it ever since. We like to serve it with all the small chunks of Green Pepper, Onion and Pineapple in it, but you can make it smooth by pureeing it. And if you want to make it more like the Chinese Restaurants do (minus the food coloring), flavor the oil with the Green Pepper and Onion and use just the Pineapple Juice to make a thinner sauce.

Sweet and Sour Sauce

2 Tablespoons Vegetable Oil

1 Green Pepper, trimmed, cut into small dice

1 Yellow Onion, diced

1 cup canned Pineapple in juice, drained (reserve juice) and cut into very small chunks

¼ cup White Balsamic Vinegar

¼ cup Sugar

3 Tablespoons Ketchup

1 Tablespoon Tamari or GF Soy Sauce

1 Tablespoon Rice Wine

2 rounded teaspoons Cornstarch

¼ cup reserved canned Pineapple Juice

In a small bowl, stir together the Vinegar, Sugar, Ketchup, Tamari and Rice Wine. In another bowl, mix together the Pineapple Juice and Cornstarch.

Heat the Oil in a frying pan. Add in the Onions and Green Peppers. Cook until the Onions are soft. Add in the diced Pineapple and then the sauce mixture. Cook until boiling. Then pour in the Pineapple Juice and Cornstarch mixture and stir until the sauce is thickened.

For Chinese Restaurant Style Sauce

Cut the Green Pepper and Onion into larger pieces.

Mix together the Vinegar, Sugar, Tamari, Rice Wine and Ketchup. In another bowl, mix together the Pineapple Juice and Cornstarch.

Heat the Oil and cook the Green Pepper and Onion until the Onion just starts to brown. Remove them from the Oil. Add in the sauce mixture and cook it just until it comes to a boil, Then, add in the Pineapple Juice and Cornstarch mixture and stir until thickened.

CHAPTER 6

Cold Plates & Salads

My Grandfather loved fresh Asparagus and this was the way I thought it tasted best. The very quick blanching leaves the Asparagus crunchy and there is just something about the dressing that works so well with the barely cooked Asparagus. You can make this dish in less than 15 minutes; the thing that takes the longest is waiting for the water to boil! Make sure not to cook the Asparagus any longer than one minute; it's really important that the Asparagus pieces remain very crisp. This salad may surprise you. It's one of our family favorites!

Chinese Asparagus Salad

1 pound of thick Asparagus Stalks, bottom inch or two cut off, then cut into thirds (preferably on a diagonal)

2 Tablespoons Tamari or GF Soy Sauce

1 Tablespoon toasted Sesame Seed Oil

1½ teaspoons Sugar

1 Tablespoon Toasted Sesame Seeds

Mix the Tamari, Sesame Oil and Sugar together in the serving bowl. Boil 4 cups water in a pot and put in the Asparagus pieces for only one minute. Drain, rinse in cold water, drain again and toss with the sauce. Refrigerate until ready to serve and then sprinkle with Sesame Seeds before serving.

Chayote is a Melon that looks like a Pear. From the bottom, it looks like a closed fist; hence it's descriptive name. Like many New World foods, it was adopted by the Chinese and is usually stir-fried. However, we like to use it raw. It has a juicy crisp texture with a flavor that is somewhat similar to Cucumber, only milder. We serve it shredded and topped with a sizzling Green Onion Salad Dressing. If you can't find Chayote, you can substitute shredded Daikon Radish.

Buddha's Hand Salad

2 Chayote Squash, peeled, cored and cut into thin shreds
4 Green Onions, trimmed and cut into small pieces
¼ cup Vegetable Oil
2 Tablespoons Tamari or GF Soy Sauce
¼ teaspoon Salt
¼ teaspoon Sugar
a pinch of White Pepper

Place Chayote Squash shreds into a serving bowl and sprinkle with Salt. Toss to combine and let it sit while making the sauce.

In a small frying pan, heat the Oil and add the Green Onion pieces. Cook until the Green Onions begin to brown on the edges. Take off the heat and add in the Tamari, Salt, Sugar and White Pepper.

Drain the Chayote shreds and then pour the sauce over it and toss to mix thoroughly.

My daughter-in-law often misses the food from her hometown and last year a Xi'an restaurant opened up nearby. One of the dishes that we ordered was a version of this Salad, so I came home and tried to make it. This recipe is the result of many attempts and it has now gotten my daughter-in-law's stamp of approval. You can replace the Daikon Radish with Bean Sprouts if you prefer. What's different about the dishes from Xi'an is the use of Cumin, which gives the more traditional Chinese-style salad dressing a bit of exotic flair.

Xi'an Carrot and Radish Salad

2 large Carrots, peeled and cut into julienned pieces about 2 inches long

2 cups Daikon Radish cut into thin shreds about 2 inches long or Bean Sprouts

2 Garlic cloves, minced

2 Tablespoons Vegetable Oil

½ teaspoon grated Ginger

½ teaspoon ground Cumin

2 Tablespoons Tamari or GF Soy Sauce

½ Tablespoon Rice Vinegar

1 teaspoon toasted Sesame Oil

1–2 teaspoons of Chili Oil

1 teaspoon Sugar

½ teaspoon Salt

Mix the Tamari, Vinegar, Sesame Oil, Chili Oil and Sugar together in a small bowl.

Put the Vegetable Oil in a frying pan and heat. Then add in the Ginger and Garlic. Cook until you can smell their fragrance. Then add in the Carrot and Daikon Radish, along with the Cumin and Salt. Cook until the Carrots and Radish pieces become slightly softened. Then add in the Tamari mixture. Stir to coat and remove from heat. Pour into a bowl and let cool to room temperature or refrigerate to serve later.

Chinese Chicken Salad is actually a Western invention based loosely on Sichuan Salads made with Chicken. This particular style of Salad became popularized starting in the 1960's with Madame Wu's restaurant and then a recipe for it was published in Sunset Magazine. Soon everyone was serving a version – even fast food restaurants!

My Mother tried it way back then and thought she could do better and to this day I think it's the best of its kind. I've tweaked it a bit over the years and I have often made it with Tofu instead of Chicken. My Mother used Iceberg Lettuce but I use Napa Cabbage instead, as it keeps better and doesn't wilt as easily. I also added Mustard to the dressing, as it helps the dressing emulsify, and also Garlic, which I think adds a depth of flavor to the dressing. And we now add Watercress leaves, which gives the salad an occasional peppery bite,

Chinese Chicken Salad can be served as a beautiful composed salad or tossed. Be sure to serve the crunchy fried Glass Noodles or Fried Tofu Shreds at the last minute, so they retain their crunch. This has been the number one requested dish whenever there is a family gathering or a potluck and we always serve it at Chinese New Year for good luck.

Lea's Chinese Chicken/Tofu Salad

DRESSING

5 Tablespoons Tamari
or GF Soy Sauce

3 Tablespoons Seasoned
Rice Vinegar

2 Tablespoons Sugar

1 Tablespoons toasted Sesame Oil

2 Tablespoons Vegetable Oil

1 teaspoon Chinese Hot Mustard
or Dijon Mustard

1 large Garlic Clove, minced
a pinch of fresh ground
White Pepper

SALAD

½ head of a small Napa Cabbage, chopped into small pieces (about 4 cups)

1 small bunch of Watercress, washed and leaves pulled off the stems

1 Red Pepper cut into thin 1-inch long strips

3 cups of shredded poached Chicken Breast or 1 block of Pressed Tofu* cut into thin strips

1 11-oz. can Mandarin Oranges, drained (you can also use a cut up large Tangerine or Navel Orange)

1 cup of blanched Snow Pea Pods or Sugar Snap Peas (strings removed)

1 Cucumber, peeled, cut in half, deseeded and cut into 1-inch long shreds

4 Green Onions, trimmed and cut into 1-inch long shreds

½ bunch Cilantro Leaves, removed from the stems

2 Tablespoons of toasted Sesame Seeds

SERVE WITH

Fried Glass Noodles and Fried Tofu Skin Threads

FOR THE DRESSING: In a large bowl, whisk together the Tamari, Seasoned Rice Vinegar, Sugar, Sesame Oil and Vegetable Oil, Garlic and Mustard. Taste and adjust seasoning and flavoring as desired. The dressing keeps for up to one week in the refrigerator.

FOR THE SALAD: In a large bowl, toss together the Napa Cabbage, Watercress, Chicken or Tofu, Cucumbers, Green Onions, Mandarin Orange pieces, Pea Pods and Red Pepper pieces along with the Cilantro leaves. Add half the dressing, tossing to lightly coat. Taste, and toss in additional dressing as desired. Sprinkle with Sesame Seeds and serve Fried Glass Noodles or Fried Tofu Skin Threads on the side to be used as individual garnishes.

*If using Tofu, slice the Tofu into thin strips. Marinate it in a mixture of 2 Tablespoons Tamari and 1 Tablespoon Rice Wine. When ready to cook, dry off the Tofu with Paper Towels. Heat a non-stick frying pan and add 1 Tablespoons of Oil. Then add Tofu shreds and pan fry until it looks dry. Cool and use in the Salad.

This is a classic Summer Chicken Salad from the Sichuan province of China. It is often translated as "Saliva Chicken" meaning that it makes your mouth water because it tastes so good. It features shredded, poached Chicken over thinly sliced Cucumbers and it is drizzled with a fiery hot dressing, which is supposed to help cool you off by making you sweat. I can't take that much Chili so I go for a much smaller amount but Stephen loves it hot, as did my Mother. The dressing is so similar to a Sichuan Soft Tofu Cold Plate that I sometimes substitute Soft Tofu instead of Chicken. I think either makes this a perfect summer lunch salad.

Sichuan Mouthwatering Chicken/Tofu Salad

DRESSING

1 – 4 Tablespoons Sichuan Chili Oil or Stephen's Crispy Chili Oil (depending on how hot you like it)

2 Tablespoons Tamari or GF Soy Sauce

2 Tablespoons Rice Vinegar

2 Tablespoons Rice Wine

1 Tablespoon toasted Sesame Oil

1 teaspoon Sugar

½ teaspoon Chicken or Vegetable Bouillon, crushed

2 large Garlic cloves, minced

FOR GARNISH

2 Green Onions, trimmed, cut into small pieces

½ cup Cilantro Leaves

1 Tablespoon Sesame Seeds

CHICKEN SALAD

1 sliced poached Chicken Breast half shredded

1 large Cucumber, ends cut off, peeled, cut in half, seeds removed and cut into 2 inch strips

TOFU SALAD

1 11-oz package of Soft (Soon) Tofu

DRESSING: Mix the Chili Oil, Tamari, Rice Vinegar, Rice Wine, Sesame Oil, Sugar, Bouillon and Garlic together.

CHICKEN SALAD: Place Cucumbers on a plate like a fan. Place the shredded Chicken on top. Drizzle the Salad Dressing over the top and sprinkle with the Green Onions, Cilantro and Sesame Seeds.

TOFU SALAD: Cut Tofu into slices and layered on a plate. Drizzle the Salad Dressing over the top and garnish with Green Onions. Cilantro or Sesame Seeds, as desired.

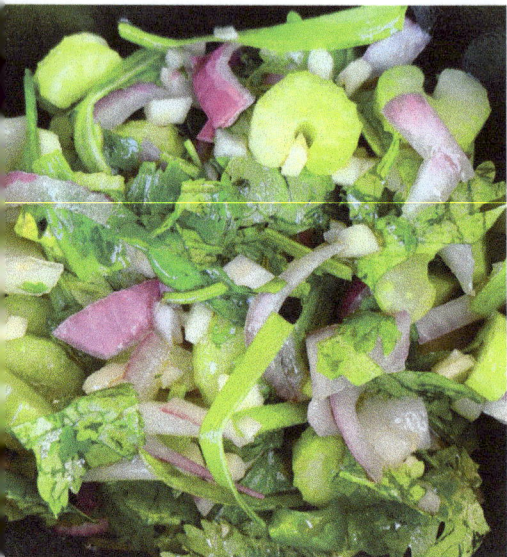

This is a bit of a strange salad in concept, but it is a classic dish in both Xi'an and across Northern China. It is really delicious and is an excellent side dish to roast meats. We especially like it piled on top of the Rou Jia Mo Sandwiches.

Xi'an Celery, Cilantro and Onion Salad

1 bunch Cilantro, washed and bottom stems cut off

3 stalks of Celery, trimmed and cut into ¼-inch wide pieces

⅓ cup of thinly sliced Red Onion, cut to match the size of the Celery

⅓ cup Green Onion tops, sliced lengthwise and then cut to match the size of the Celery

1 Garlic Clove, minced

1 Tablespoon Chili Oil

1 Tablespoon toasted Sesame Oil

1 Tablespoon Tamari or GF Soy Sauce

½ Tablespoon Rice Vinegar

1 teaspoon Sugar

In a small bowl, pour in 1 cup of Boiling Water and add ½ teaspoon of Salt. Add the Red Onion and let soak for 10 minutes

In another bowl, mix together the Garlic, the Chili Oil, the Sesame Oil, the Tamari the Vinegar and the Sugar. Stir to combine.

Drain the Red Onion and put into a large serving bowl with the Celery, Green Onions and Cilantro. Pour the sauce over the vegetables and stir to mix thoroughly. Let the Salad sit for at least 15 minutes for the flavors to meld or refrigerate until ready to serve. Toss before serving.

Chinese Cucumber Salads

Cucumber is considered a cooling food in Chinese Medicine and therefore it is a perfect dish for summer or whenever you serve other dishes that are spicy hot. Every region in China and every home cook have slightly different sauces to serve over their Cucumbers and all are delicious. The difference in the sauce ingredients is not as interesting as the various ways that Cucumbers can be cut. Most of the time, Cucumbers are peeled and deseeded before slicing and then cubed or sliced. However, when using small Persian style Cucumbers, they can also be smashed, which helps the sauce to be absorbed. Since all Cucumber Salads contain some Vinegar, they are good when served with fried foods or fatty meats to aid digestion. We are offering three versions of Cucumber Salad that are favorites in our family.

This is an adaptation of my Grandfather, Kingway Lowe's Cucumber Salad and I still make this regularly. It's great as one of several Chinese dishes, especially when served with fatty foods. It has been quite a popular dish whenever I have been invited to a potluck, as it keeps well if made ahead and can even be kept overnight. But if you don't eat it right away, the Cucumbers do become softer and more like pickles and then we use them on Rou Jia Mo Sandwiches.

Lowe Family Cucumber Salad

2 large Cucumbers

1 large or 2 small Garlic cloves, minced

2 Tablespoons Seasoned Rice Wine Vinegar (or 2 Tablespoons Rice Vinegar and 2 teaspoons Sugar)

2 Tablespoons toasted Sesame Oil

1 teaspoon coarse Sea Salt – divided

OPTIONAL

1/2 teaspoon or more of Chili Oil

FOR SERVING

1 teaspoon toasted Sesame Seeds

Peel Cucumbers and cut in half. Scrape out the seeds with small spoon and then slice into ¼-inch half-moons or cut in half lengthwise and then into 1-inch chunks cut at an angle. Put into bowl and sprinkle with ½ teaspoon Salt. Let the Cucumbers sit for 10 minutes and then drain. Add in the Garlic, Seasoned Rice Vinegar, Sesame Oil, and remaining ½ teaspoon Salt and Chili Oil, if using. Stir to mix. Taste to adjust seasoning, as desired. Sprinkle with Sesame Seeds when ready to serve. This salad can be made ahead and refrigerated. The longer it sits, the more the Cucumbers get pickled and soften.

You will find a version of this Cucumber Salad all over China and because of the many Sichuan restaurants in America, it has become a favorite. This was my Mother's way of making Sichuan Cucumber Salad. She loved the spicy and numbing Mala flavors of Sichuan Chili Oil combined with Sichuan Peppercorns, which blend perfectly with cool, crunchy and juicy Cucumbers.

Sichuan Smashed Cucumber Salad

4 Persian Cucumbers or
1 large Hothouse Cucumber

2 large Garlic cloves minced

2 Tablespoons toasted Sesame Oil

1 Tablespoon Stephen's Crispy
Chili Oil with the Chili bits

1 teaspoon Sichuan Chili Oil

1 Tablespoon Rice Vinegar

1 teaspoon Sichuan Peppercorn
Salt or Salt–divided

1 teaspoon Sugar

Trim the ends off the Cucumber and using a large heavy knife (or a coffee mug) smash the Cucumbers lightly until the skin breaks. Cut into ½-inch wide

sections. Place in a bowl with the Garlic, ½ of the Salt and Sugar and toss. In a small bowl, mix together the Sesame Oil, Crispy Chili Oil, remaining ½ teaspoon Salt and Vinegar. Pour over Cucumbers and toss to mix. Refrigerate at least 15 minutes up until overnight. Sprinkle with Sichuan Chili Oil before serving.

This Cucumber Salad has the wonderful flavors of Ginger and Tamari with a hint of Bay Leaf too. It is my daughter-in-law's favorite Cucumber Salad, so we make it often. If there are any Cucumbers left over, they make wonderful pickles for Rou Jia Mo Sandwiches. So, we usually double or triple the recipe whenever we make this delicious Cucumber Salad!

Tamari Ginger Cucumber Salad

4 Persian Cucumbers trimmed and sliced into rounds, or 2 regular Cucumbers, peeled, seeded and cut into half moon slices–equal to 3 cups when sliced

1 teaspoon Salt

3 Tablespoons Tamari or GF Soy Sauce

2 Tablespoons Sugar

2 Tablespoons Rice Vinegar

2 cloves Garlic, minced

½ teaspoon grated Ginger

2 Bay Leaves, broken in half

Place the Cucumbers in a bowl and sprinkle with ½ teaspoon Salt. Mix well with your hands and let sit for 15 minutes. Drain the liquid. Then in a small bowl, mix together the Tamari, Sugar, Vinegar, Ginger and Garlic. Pour over the Cucumbers and add the Bay Leaves and mix well. Place in a covered container and refrigerate until ready to serve. Remove the Bay Leaves before serving.

My daughter-in-law loves Eggplant in almost any manifestation and this is one of her favorite Eggplant dishes. Traditionally, the Eggplant for this kind of dish is steamed, but we think roasting gives it more depth of flavor. We like to serve this as a dip with Rice Crackers.

Eggplant Cold Plate

12 Chinese or Japanese Eggplants
2 Tablespoons Vegetable Oil
1 teaspoon Garlic, minced
1 teaspoon grated Ginger
1 Tablespoon Tamari or GF Soy Sauce
1 Tablespoon Rice Vinegar
1 teaspoon Sugar
2 Tablespoons Sesame Seeds
2 Green Onions, trimmed and minced
a pinch of Salt

Heat the oven to 400°F. Pierce each eggplant several times and place on a baking sheet and bake for about 45 minutes or until very soft when pierced with a fork. Cool and then pull off the skin and chop the Eggplant.

Toast the Sesame Seeds in a small frying pan until golden, remove from the pan and put on a plate to cool off. Then add the Oil to the pan. Stir in the Garlic and Ginger and cook until you can smell the fragrance. Add in the Tamari and Vinegar and Sugar. Pour over the Eggplant and mix thoroughly. Refrigerate to let the flavors meld before serving. Sprinkle with Sesame Seeds before serving.

Enoki Mushrooms, also called Golden Needles or Lily Mushrooms, have always looked like sea creatures to me, as they have long thin stems and a little tiny cap. They appear to be very delicate, but have a surprisingly al dente texture, even when blanched. Because they have such a mild taste, they can handle a strongly flavored sauce and they taste even better when they marinate for a while.

Enoki Mushroom Cold Plate

3 packages of Enoki Mushrooms (about 7 ounces each)
2 Tablespoons of Vegetable Oil
3 Garlic cloves, minced
2 Green Onions, trimmed and cut into small pieces
3 Tablespoons Tamari or GF Soy Sauce
½ teaspoon Sugar
1 teaspoon toasted Sesame Oil

In a small bowl, mix together the Tamari, Sugar, Salt and Sesame Oil.

Trim off the bottom one inch of the Enoki Mushrooms and rinse. Heat a small pot or frying pan filled with water to a boil. Put in the Enoki Mushrooms and blanch for about 40 seconds. Remove with tongs and place on a platter with the Enoki Mushrooms all facing the same direction. Drain any remaining water off the plate and pull apart the bottom of the mushrooms so that the mushrooms are mostly separated.

In a small frying pan, heat the Oil and add the Garlic cloves and the Green Onion pieces. Cook until you can smell the fragrance. Pour in the Tamari Mixture and cook until it starts to bubble. Pour over the Mushrooms. You can serve this dish warm or refrigerate and serve cold.

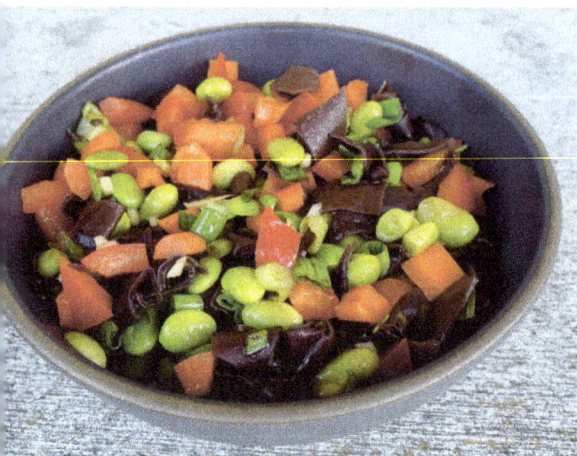

Mu'er Mushrooms, often called Wood Ear Mushrooms, are an odd ingredient, but a very healthy one. They have no real taste and they are mostly known for their texture, which is rubbery and crunchy at the same time. I try to find many ways to eat them, as they are considered good for the blood and the heart and this salad is one of my favorite ways to incorporate them into my diet. Combined with Soybeans, Red Pepper, Carrot and Green Onions, this salad is colorful and delicious!

Mu'er Mushroom and Soybean Salad

1 cup of dried Mu'er (Dried Black Fungus or Wood Ear Mushroom)

½ cup diced Carrot pieces

Boiling Water

2 cloves of Garlic, minced

½ cup diced Red Pepper

½ cup cooked green Soybeans (Edamame)

3 Green Onions, green part only, cut into small pieces

1 Tablespoon Rice Vinegar

1 Tablespoon Tamari or GF Soy Sauce

1 teaspoon toasted Sesame Oil

½ teaspoon Chili Oil

1 teaspoon Sugar

Place Mu'er and Carrot pieces in a large bowl and cover with Boiling Water. Soak until the Mu'er pieces are soft. Then drain in a colander and wash the Mu'er and Carrots with cold water, removing any grit from the Mu'er. Tear the Mu'er into bite size pieces, cutting away any hard pieces. Shake dry and place back in a serving bowl with the other vegetables. In a small bowl, whisk together the dressing ingredients and pour over the salad. Toss to coat. Refrigerate for at least 30 minutes, tossing at least once.

Potatoes are not traditionally associated with Chinese cuisine, although like all New World foods, it has become a staple ingredient. Chinese chefs barely cook Potatoes so they are not at all starchy. Chinese Potato Salad is always served cold, which really means room temperature. Potatoes and slivers of Carrot are slightly blanched in salted water to maintain their crunch and are then tossed with the Dressing. It actually takes longer to cut the vegetables than it does to cook them. This Chinese version of Potato Salad will probably surprise you. It's beautiful and delicious!

Chinese Potato Salad

4 medium Red Potatoes, peeled
1 Carrot, trimmed and peeled
Water for blanching
½ cup of loosely packed Cilantro Leaves
1½ Tablespoons Rice Vinegar
1½ Tablespoons Tamari or GF Soy Sauce
2 Tablespoons toasted Sesame Oil
½ teaspoon Sugar

Cut the Potatoes and Carrots into ¼-inch thick slices and then cut again into thin shreds. Heat a small pot of water and when it is boiling, add in the Potato and Carrots pieces. Cook for 2 minutes. Drain and rinse with cold water and place in a serving bowl.

In a small bowl, mix together the Vinegar, Tamari, Sesame Oil and Sugar. Pour over the Potatoes and Carrots and toss to combine. Sprinkle with Cilantro. Toss several more times before serving.

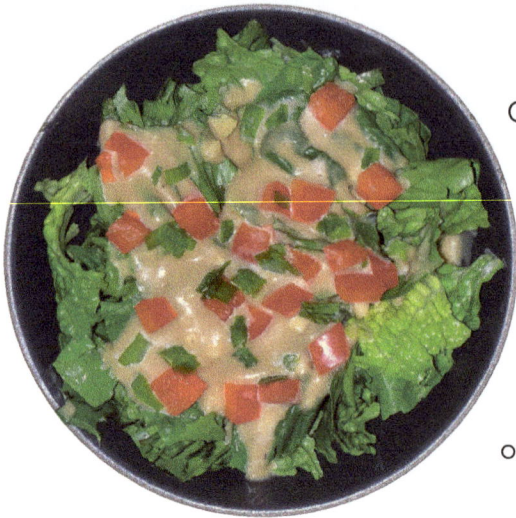

One of our local Dim Sum restaurants serves an A Choi Salad with Sesame Dressing that is delicious. So, we had to figure out how to make our own version. Since A Choi is hard to find, we decided to use Romaine Lettuce. The only difficulty with this dressing is that the different Sesame Pastes you can buy all have a different consistency. So, you will have to thin yours with enough Hot Water or Broth until it pours like a salad dressing. This Salad is so delicious and addictive that you will find yourself making it over and over again!

Sesame Romaine Salad

4 cups cut up Romaine Lettuce

¼ cup Red Bell Pepper, cut into small pieces

2 Tablespoons minced Green Onion Tops

OPTIONAL

¼ cup blanched Green Beans, cut into small pieces

Place the Romaine Lettuce in a Salad Bowl and top with the Red Bell Pepper, Green Onions and Green Beans, if using. Drizzle the Sesame Salad Dressing over the Salad and toss to coat thoroughly.

SESAME SALAD DRESSING

½ cup Chinese Sesame Paste or Tahini

¼ cup hot Chicken or Vegetable Broth

1–3 Tablespoons Hot Water, if necessary

2 Tablespoons low sodium Tamari or GF Soy Sauce

1 Tablespoon Rice Vinegar

1–1½ Tablespoons toasted Sesame Oil

1 Tablespoon Sugar

2 Garlic cloves, minced

½–1 teaspoon Salt

OPTIONAL

¼–1 teaspoon Chili Oil

Mix together the Sesame Paste or Tahini with the Hot Broth. Stir with a whisk until completely smooth. Then add in the Tamari, Rice Vinegar, Sesame Oil, Sugar, Salt, Garlic and Chili Oil, if using. Stir until well blended. Taste and adjust Sesame Oil and Salt as desired and thin the sauce to the desired consistency by adding Hot Water.

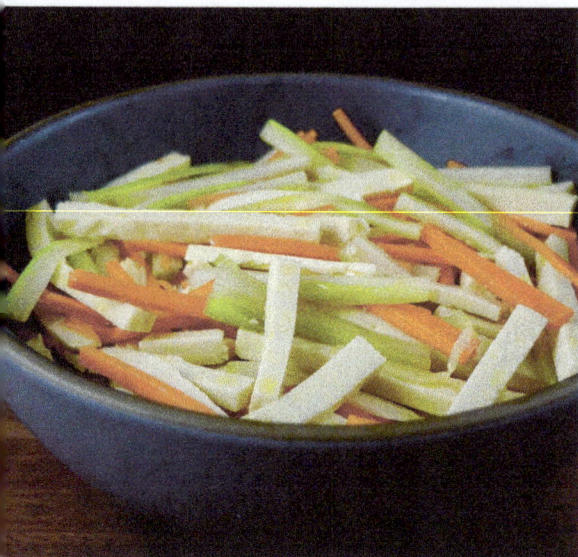

This is a simple and delicious salad that is often served at Chinese restaurants. It is lightly seasoned with toasted Sesame Oil, Salt, Sugar and sometimes Sichuan Pepper or Chili Oil. We use homemade pressed Tofu cut into shreds, but you can also buy already pressed Tofu at an Asian market and sometimes you can even find Tofu Noodles already cut up. We've always loved this salad and make it frequently. You can make it spicier with more Chili Oil and you can add some Green Onion shreds if you like too. This Tofu Strip Salad has convinced a lot of our friends that Tofu can taste good!

Tofu Strip Salad with Carrots and Celery

2 large stalks of Celery, trimmed, cut into 2-inch julienned pieces (about 1 cup)

2 large Carrots, trimmed, peeled, cut into 2-inch julienned pieces (about 1 cup)

1 piece of Pressed Tofu, sliced into thin shreds (about 1½ cups) or Tofu Noodles

¼ cup toasted Sesame Oil

2 Tablespoons Vegetable Oil

1 teaspoon Fine Sea Salt, Sichuan Pepper Salt or Chili Salt

½ teaspoon Sugar

OPTIONAL

1 – 2 Tablespoons Sichuan Chili Oil (replacing the Vegetable Oil)

OPTIONAL

1 – 2 Green Onions, green tops only, sliced very thin vertically and cut into 2-inch long pieces

Put the Celery, Carrot and Tofu Strips in a large bowl. Cover with boiling water and let soften for a few minutes. Drain thoroughly and toss with the Sesame Oil, Vegetable Oil, Salt and Sugar and Chili Oil (if using). Drizzle on more Chili Oil, if desired and add the Green Onions, if using. Refrigerate until cold.

CHAPTER 7

Dim Sum Favorites

Dim Sum is a classic Chinese dining experience, where delicious small plates of food are wheeled around on carts and diners can pick and choose whatever dishes they want to try. Dim Sum is always served with lots of Tea. It's exciting to see cart after cart filled with different kinds of Bao, and Chinese Pastries, but they are traditionally made with wheat. We are offering Gluten Free versions of these treats.

Char Siu Bao are steamed yeasted buns and Pastry Puffs are baked. Dumplings, however, are the star of the Dim Sum show and are also one of the most beloved foods of China. They come stuffed with a variety of fillings and can be boiled, steamed, pan-fried and even deep-fried. Jiaozi are boiled dumplings; Guotie are Potstickers; Xi'an Bing are pan-fried dumplings, often called Meat Pies; Xiao Long Bao are the famous steamed Shanghai Soup dumplings; and Sesame Rice Balls are deep fried. Dumplings are so important to the Chinese that they are always served at Chinese New Year as a symbol of good luck, representing gold and silver.

Char Siu Bao are a Dim Sum staple. They are soft, steamed buns usually filled with Pork, often leftover Char Siu Pork, that has been added to a sweetened sauce. We never have any leftover Char Siu Pork, so we offer a slightly tangier Pork, Chicken or Tofu filling. You can also use any of the other Dumpling Fillings instead. Try Sweet Red Bean Paste as a dessert filling. We have found that it's helpful to freeze the filling in small cupcake tins and then mold the dough around the frozen filling. Be sure to place the Buns on squares of waxed paper when you steam them so that they are not in direct contact with the heat. Char Slu Bao takes some time to make, but they freeze well, so you can have them any time you want!

Char Siu Bao

CHAR SIU BAO FILLING

1 pound diced Pork Tenderloin, Chicken Thighs or firm pressed Tofu

1 Shallot, minced or Onions (about ⅓ cup)

1 Tablespoon of Oil

¼ cup Mushroom Tamari or GF Soy Sauce

¼ cup Rice Wine

¼ cup Chicken or Vegetable Broth

1 Tablespoons Ketchup

2 Tablespoons Sugar

1 Tablespoon of Cornstarch mixed with 2 Tablespoons of Water

Mix the Tamari, Rice Wine, Chicken or Vegetable Broth, Ketchup and Sugar together in a small bowl. Mix the Cornstarch in another small bowl.

Heat Oil in a frying pan and add in the Shallots. Cook until you smell the fragrance. Then add in the Pork, Chicken or Tofu. Cook until the meat is no longer pink or the Tofu just starts to brown. Add in the sauce mixture and bring to a boil. Reduce heat and add in the Cornstarch mixture. Cook until thickened. Cool before using as a filling or place rounded Tablespoons of the filling into a small cupcake tin and freeze until firm.

CHAR SIU BAO DOUGH

2½ cups White Rice Flour	1 teaspoon Baking Powder
1 packet of Active Dry Yeast (2¼ teaspoons)	¼ cup Lard or Vegetable Shortening
¾ cup warm Water	2 teaspoons Xanthan Gum
1 Tablespoon Sugar	¼ cup Cilantro leaves for garnish
½ teaspoon Salt	Cut wax paper into 8 4-inch squares

In a large bowl, combine 2 ¼ cups of the Rice Flour, Xanthan Gum, Salt and Lard or Vegetable Shortening. Put aside. In another bowl, dissolve Yeast and Sugar in Warm Water. Wait until little bubbles start to form. Add to the Rice Flour and stir until it comes together in a ball. Put in a warm place and let rise for about 45 minutes. Then add in some of additional of the additional ¼ cup of Rice Flour to make the dough the consistency of Playdoh. If it becomes too dry, add in 1 Tablespoon of Water at a time to moisten.

Take about ¼ cup of Rice Dough and form into a ball. Place on a cutting board sprinkled with a little Rice Flour. Then flatten the dough as thin as you can make it and place one heaping Tablespoon of Char Siu Bao Filling in the center. Bring the sides up to seal, using extra dough to seal any tears. Place the filled Bao seam side down on a piece of wax paper. Place in a steamer basket with a little space in between each bun. Steam for 20 minutes.

To reheat, cover a Bao with a wet paper towel and cook in a microwave for 30 seconds to 1 minute.

Makes 8

Dumplings are one of my favorite foods and I was determined to create a really good Gluten Free Dumpling Dough. It was much harder than I thought and it took me over a year of trial and error before I got it right. It had to work for Boiled and Steamed and Pan-Fried Dumplings too. I tried so many different combinations of flours and was about to give up and then this recipe came to me first thing one morning, fully formed and I quickly wrote it down. Later that day I made the recipe and to my delight the Dumplings were perfect! I actually cried from happiness. This recipe works every time. I usually make extra Dumplings and freeze some, so I always have some on hand. You can now make wonderfully crisp Potstickers and soft, succulent Boiled or Steamed Dumplings that are Gluten Free!

Dumpling Wrapper Dough

1 cup Rice Flour
¾ cup Tapioca Starch
+ ½ cup more for rolling
¼ cup Sticky Rice Flour

1 teaspoon Salt
2 Teaspoons Xanthan Gum
2 Tablespoons Vegetable Oil
1 cup Boiling Water

Sprinkle ¼ cup of Tapioca Starch on a cutting board.

Mix together the Rice Flour, Tapioca Starch and Sticky Rice Flour with the Salt and Xanthan Gum. Pour in the Oil and the Boiling Water and mix thoroughly.

Put onto the cutting board and knead lightly, incorporating the Tapioca Starch to keep the dough from being sticky. Cover with plastic wrap and let sit for 30 minutes.

Then sprinkle some additional Tapioca Starch on the cutting board. Cut dough into four sections. Roll out one piece of dough until it is about ¼ inch thick. Cut circles out with a 3-inch round biscuit cutter. Reserve scraps. Repeat with next piece of dough until all the Wrappers have been cut. Then reform the remaining scraps to cut out any additional Wrappers.

Makes 36 3-inch Wrappers

Filling Dumplings

Lay each wrapper down and place 1 Tablespoon of the filling of your choice on the top-side of the center. Fold the wrapper over from the bottom nearest you to make a half moon shape. Pinch tightly to seal the edges. Cook the dumplings immediately or freeze for future use. You can cook frozen dumplings, just be sure to cook them a bit longer.

Cooking Dumplings

FOR POTSTICKERS: Put 2 Tablespoons of Vegetable Oil in a 10 or 12-inch frying pan (with a lid) and add just enough Dumplings so that none are touching. Cook until the bottom is browned, then turn them over to another side. Pour in ½ cup of Chicken or Vegetable Broth and cover (do not lower the heat). Cook until the Broth almost completely evaporates. Take the cover off, push the Potstickers around the pan a bit and crisp them back up. Put the Potstickers on a plate to cool. Repeat with next batch until all Potstickers are cooked. Serve with the Dumpling Dipping Sauce of your choice.

FOR BOILED DUMPLINGS: Heat a large pot with 2 cups of Chicken or Vegetable Broth and 2 cups of Water and bring it to a boil. Add the Dumplings and return to a boil. Lower heat and cook for 7 minutes. Drain and serve with the Dumpling Dipping Sauce of your choice.

FOR STEAMED DUMPLINGS: Place Napa Cabbage Leaves on top of a bamboo steamer basket or metal steamer tray. Put the Dumplings on top, keeping them from touching. Place over water boiling in a Wok or a Pot. Steam for 15 minutes. Serve with the Dumpling Sauce of your choice.

Xi'an Bing are often called Meat Pies. They are pan-fried discs of dough that are usually stuffed with a meat filling. We came up with a Gluten Free and Grain Free Dough made from Potato Starch and Sweet Potato Starch that is easy to work with. We were inspired by the Ba Wan Dumplings of Taiwan made with Sweet Potato Starch and the Glass or Crystal Dumplings that use Potato Starch and Wheat Starch. We put those two starches together and came up with this dough. We like to make the Bing on the small side – about 3 inches-inch wide, but you can certainly make them bigger.

You can actually use any of the dumpling fillings to make Xi'an Bing and it's easy to fill them; you don't even have to roll out the dough. You just press it into a circle, reserving a small piece of dough, put in the filling mixture, pull up the dough and place that small piece (flattened) across the top to seal it. Then you pan-fry it just like Potstickers, although in this case you use water to steam them. They turn out crispy, very chewy and delicious!

Xi'an Bing Dough

1½ cups Potato Starch + more for the cutting board
1½ cups Sweet Potato Starch
1 teaspoon Salt
2 cups Boiling Hot Water
3 Tablespoons Vegetable Oil

In a large bowl, mix together the Potato Starch, Sweet Potato Starch and Salt. Add the water and the Vegetable Oil and stir to combine. Then use your hands to knead the dough. Cover the dough with plastic wrap and let rest for 15 minutes.

Sprinkle some Potato Starch on a cutting board. Cut the dough into 24 pieces and make into balls. Cover with a damp paper towel.

Taking one ball of dough, pinch off about 1 teaspoon and put aside. Then press the ball of dough with your finger on your cutting sheet into about a 4-inch circle.

Filling dumplings

Make 1 recipe of Dumpling Filling of your choice. Place about 2 Tablespoons of filling in the center of the circle of dough and flatten the filling slightly. Pull the dough up and over the sides, leaving about a one-inch circle uncovered. Take the reserved piece of dough and press into a circle slightly larger than the opening and press down over the opening to seal.

Place on a plate and repeat the process until all the Bing are filled. You may have extra filling. The Bing can now be frozen for later or cooked.

Cooking Xi'an Bing

Place 2 Tablespoons of oil in a large non-stick frying pan. Heat on medium high and then add in as many Bing as you can comfortably fit without them touching, the patched side down. Cook until they just start to brown and turn over. Cook until that side slightly browns. Then turn back over, add ½ cup of water, cover the pan and cook for 5–6 minutes on medium heat or until all the water has evaporated. Take the lid off and turn the heat back up to medium high and crisp until browned. Turn the Bing over and place on a plate.

Many of my friends are following the Ketogenic Diet, so I created another way for them to still enjoy the filling of Dumplings without wrappers made from grains. The trick is to stuff Zucchini or Shitake Mushrooms and then pan braise them. You could very easily branch out and stuff the fillings into mini Pepper halves, or between two Eggplant slices or Lotus Root. Any way you make them, they are delicious!

Keto Dumplings

STUFFED ZUCCHINI

4 medium Zucchini, ends trimmed and cut crosswise into 1½ inch rounds

Scoop out the center of each Zucchini with a small spoon, leaving about ¼ inch on the sides and ½-inch on the bottom. Stuff the Zucchini as directed below.

STUFFED SHITAKE MUSHROOMS

20 large fresh Shitake Mushrooms washed, or 20 dried Shitake Mushroom soaked in boiling water for 1 hour.

Remove as much of the stem as you can and then stuff as directed below.

Filling Dumplings

Fill each piece of Zucchini or Shitake Mushrooms with the Meat or Tofu Filling of your choice. Flatten and smooth the stuffing lightly with the curved part of the spoon

Cooking Dumplings

2 Tablespoons Vegetable Oil

½ – ¾ cup Chicken or Vegetable Broth
(use more for Shitake Mushrooms)

1 Tablespoon Tamari or GF Soy Sauce

¼ teaspoon toasted Sesame Oil

1 teaspoon Cornstarch mixed
with 1 Tablespoon of Water

1 Green Onion (green part only),
 cut into small pieces

Heat the Oil in a frying pan and arrange the Stuffed Zucchini or Shitake Mushrooms stuffing side down and fry for 2 minutes or until browned. Reduce heat, turn them stuffing side up and add Broth and Tamari. Cover and simmer for five minutes. Remove to a serving plate.

Mix Cornstarch and Water. Add to the pan and cook on medium heat until the Sauce thickens. Then add in the Sesame Oil and pour the Sauce over and sprinkle with Green Onion pieces to serve.

Dumpling and Bing Fillings

Dumplings are one of the most famous foods from China and they are always served at Chinese New Year. There are so many different kinds of fillings and you can literally fill them with almost anything! We are giving you several of our family's favorite fillings. No matter which filling you use, you might want to double the recipe for the filling and the wrappers so you can freeze any extras. They are just so good that you will end up wanting to eat more soon!

This first dumpling filling comes from my Grandfather and he usually used Pork. We like to use a combination of ground Pork and Chicken together so that they are a bit lighter. For our Vegetarian and Vegan friends, we make these with Tofu and you can also use Bok Choy or regular Cabbage instead. We also give you a version using Chinese Chives. If you want to make Dumplings Xi'an Style, use ground Lamb, omit the Sesame Oil and add some ground Cumin.

Lowe Family Filling

1 pound ground Pork, ground Chicken or ½ of each, or Firm Tofu, crumbled

4 cups minced Napa Cabbage leaves (or Bok Choy or regular Cabbage)

3–4 Green Onions, trimmed and sliced into small pieces

3 Tablespoons Tamari or GF Soy Sauce (use more for Tofu)

2 Tablespoons toasted Sesame Oil

Place Napa Cabbage in a large mixing bowl. Squeeze to release extra moisture and blot it up with a clean paper towel. Then add in the other ingredients. Mix thoroughly with your hands in a large bowl.

Pork/Chicken/Tofu and Chinese Chives Filling

1 pound ground Pork, Chicken or Firm Tofu, crumbled

2 cups minced Chinese Chives (bottom 1-inch removed before mincing)

2 Tablespoons Tamari

1 Tablespoon Rice Wine

1 Tablespoon toasted Sesame Oil

1 teaspoon grated Ginger

Mix all ingredients thoroughly in a mixing bowl with your hands so all the Chives are incorporated.

I was in Germany for one Chinese New Year and I wanted to make Dumplings. I couldn't find Napa Cabbage and I didn't want to use winter Green Cabbage because it just looked a little too tough. So, I created a filling with Spinach along with minced Chicken and Shitake Mushrooms that was so good, I've been making it ever since. I actually think it tastes better if you take the time to mince the Chicken with a cleaver or a big Chef's knife, but ground Chicken is a lot faster and just as tasty!

Chicken, Spinach and Shitake Filling

1 pound of Spinach, stems removed, washed and chopped finely

½ pound of Chicken, minced fine (or ground)

6 Shitake Mushrooms, rehydrated in a small amount of boiling water, stems removed and minced fine

½ of a small Onion, minced fine

2 cloves Garlic, minced fine

2 Tablespoons Tamari or GF Soy Sauce

1 teaspoon toasted Sesame Oil

¼ teaspoon Sugar

¼ teaspoon Salt

⅛ teaspoon White Pepper

Mix all ingredients together thoroughly in a bowl with your hands. Use to stuff Dumplings.

Chinese Chives were an acquired taste for me, but not because of how they taste. It was because I was afraid to eat dumplings made from them because the smell was so strong. But I learned that the taste of cooked Chinese Chives is actually quite mild. Stephen and I developed this recipe after visiting many famous Dumpling restaurants (when we still ate wheat) and we wanted to recreate what was called Leek Dumplings. I knew that Leek also means Chinese Chives to the Chinese, so we decided to make a filling that was even more complex by adding real Leeks along with Green Onions to make a wonderful Dumpling Filling. Sometimes we also add Glass Noodles and Scrambled Eggs and that's a great filling too. I think this Dumpling Filling will surprise you!

Chinese Chive, Leek and Green Onion Filling

2 cups finely chopped Chinese Garlic Chives (trim off hard ends)

1 Leek, dark green part cut off, cut in quarters, washed and sliced thinly

3 Green Onions, trimmed and cut into small pieces

1 Tablespoon of Oil

½ teaspoon Salt

½ teaspoon Sugar

A few drops toasted Sesame Oil

A pinch of Baking Soda

OPTIONAL

2 ounces of Glass Noodles, rehydrated in boiling water and cut into small pieces

2 Eggs, very lightly scrambled

Heat a frying pan with 1 Tablespoon of Oil. Add in the Garlic Chives, Leeks and Green Onions. Cook until softened. Add in the Salt, Sugar, Sesame Oil and Baking Powder and mix thoroughly. If using Glass Noodles and Scrambled Eggs, add them now. Let the mixture cool. Then drain the accumulated liquid and use as a Dumpling Filling.

These are the famous and magical dumplings from Shanghai that contain a bit of soup in them that bursts out when you bite into them. Stephen and I love these dumplings so much that we had to find a way to make them Gluten Free. Luckily our basic Dumpling Dough can also be used for Xiao Long Bao, the wrapper will not be as delicate as the ones made with wheat, they will still taste wonderful!

The filling is ground Pork with an Aspic mixed in that is made ahead of time. The Aspic is jellied soup, as it's made from Pork Skin along with Chicken. This Aspic is added to ground Pork and when the dumpling is steamed, the Aspic melts and becomes delicious soup inside the Dumpling.

It's important to make these wrappers a bit bigger than for Potstickers, as you have to make sure that the filling is completely encased or the soup will leak out. We like to cut the dough into 4-inch squares and make them into little 4-pointed pouches, but you can also make them round if you prefer. Remember to bite into these dumplings very carefully so you don't burn yourself. These dumplings are so delicious that you won't be able to stop eating them!

Xiao Long Bao – Shanghai Soup Filling

ASPIC

1 pound of Chicken Drumsticks or Thighs (can also use Chicken Bones)

½ pound Pork Skin or Pork Belly with Skin

4 Green Onions, trimmed, white part only (reserve the green tops for the filling)

3 slices of Ginger

4 cups Water

2 teaspoons Salt

1 teaspoons of Gelatin

Place Chicken and Pork Skin into a pot with the Green Onions, Ginger and Rice Wine. Pour water over and bring to a boil. Reduce heat to simmer where bubbles show and skim the foam frequently. Cook until the liquid is reduced by half, approximately 2 hours. Strain the stock and place into a glass container. You should have about 2 cups. Taste and add more Salt if desired.

Sprinkle with the Gelatin and whisk it in thoroughly. Refrigerate overnight. When ready to use, scrape off the fat congealed on top and cut up the Aspic into small pieces by running a fork through it or chop it up with a knife into ¼ inch chunks.

XIAO LONG BAO FILLING

2 pounds of Ground Pork or Chicken

4 Green Onions – green parts only, cut into small pieces

2 teaspoons grated Ginger

¼ cup Tamari or GF Soy Sauce

¼ cup Rice Wine

2 Tablespoons of toasted Sesame Oil

1½ cups of Aspic, cut up into small pieces

Mix together the Ground Pork or Chicken, Green Onion, Ginger, Tamari, Rice Wine and Sesame Oil. Then add in the Aspic and mix lightly. Place in the freezer to keep cold until ready to use.

Use a double recipe of Gluten Free Dumpling Dough and cut into 4-inch squares. Place 2 Tablespoons of the filling in the center and bring up the two points of the dough and pinch to close. Then bring up the other two points and pinch them all together in the center and then close the 3 seams. You should have a little pouch with 4 points. Or, you can press the seams down to make a ball. Patch any tears with additional dough if necessary. Lay Napa Cabbage leaves down in the steamer or use steamer liners. Place the Dumplings on top. Cook over boiling water for 15 minutes. Serve with Dumpling Dipping Sauces.

TO EAT: pick up the Xiao Long Bao with a pair of chopsticks and place on a Chinese Soup Spoon (either ceramic or plastic). Spoon some of the Dumpling Dipping Sauce over the Xiao Long Bao. Bring the spoon up to your mouth and bite off a little piece of the Dumpling wrapper and drink up the soup carefully. Then eat the Dumpling!

When I was a little girl, we used to go to Chinatown and one of my favorite places to go was the Chinese Bakery. Since I love savory foods more than sweet, I was always drawn to the Curry Puffs. I found them on Dim Sum carts too. So, we created Curry Puffs with a Gluten Free pastry dough. We usually stuff them with Curried Beef, but Curried Chicken or Tofu are delicious options. We also gave you one more variation, my current favorite, Shanghai Radish filling. If you can find frozen Gluten Free Puff Pastry, that's an easy shortcut. If you want to make these Vegan, omit the Egg and use a Vegan Egg Replacement. You can also use the Char Siu Filling. We think these make great party appetizers!

Dim Sum Baked Pastry Puffs

GLUTEN FREE PASTRY DOUGH

1½ cups Gluten-Free Flour Blend *(See recipe on page 27)*

2 teaspoons Xanthan Gum (if the Flour Blend does not include it)

½ cup cold Lard
or Vegetable Shortening
2 teaspoons Sugar
1 teaspoon Baking Powder

½ teaspoon Sea Salt
1 large Egg
or Vegan Egg Replacement
⅓ cup Ice Water

FOR BAKING

1 additional Egg lightly beaten, for Egg Wash

In a food processor (or large mixing bowl), mix together the GF Flour, Sugar, Baking Powder and Salt. Then add in Lard (or Shortening). Pulse until it is incorporated (or use a pastry cutter or two forks). Then add in the Egg and Cold Water and mix until it forms a ball. Wrap in plastic and chill until cold (about 30 minutes).

Heat oven to 350°. Then lightly dust a cutting board and rolling pin with a little extra GF Flour. Roll out ½ of the dough at a time and cut 4- inch squares with a cookie cutter. Use a dough scraper to lift the dough. Place one piece in the palm of your hand. Fill with 1 slightly rounded Tablespoon of filling and pinch to seal. Place on a parchment or silicone mat covered baking sheet. Repeat until all are filled. Use a little extra dough if needed to patch any tears. Brush with Egg Wash. Bake for 15–20 minutes or until golden brown.

CURRY BEEF/CHICKEN FILLING

½ pound Ground Beef
or Ground Chicken

½ cup of minced Onion

2 Tablespoons Curry Powder

1 Tablespoon Tamari
or GF Soy Sauce

⅓ cup Chicken or Vegetable Broth

2 teaspoons of Cornstarch mixed
with 1½ Tablespoons Water

Add the Ground Beef or Chicken and Onion to a frying pan. Cook until
the Beef or Chicken in no longer pink and drain the fat. Add in the Curry
Powder and Tamari and stir to mix well. Then add in the Broth and the
Cornstarch mixture, stirring until thickened. Place in a covered container and
refrigerate until cold.

CURRY TOFU FILLING

1 14-oz package Firm or
Extra Firm Tofu

2 Tablespoons Tamari
or GF Soy Sauce

2 Tablespoons Curry Powder

2 Tablespoons Vegetable Oil

1 small Onion, minced
(about ½ cup)

¼ cup minced Carrot

¼ cup minced Celery

Crumble the Tofu in bowl.
Add the Tamari and Curry
Powder and mix well.

Add the oil to a frying pan and heat. Then add in the Onion, Carrots and
Celery. Cook until soft. Then add in the Tofu and cook until the Tofu is hot.
Place in a covered container and refrigerate until the filling is cool.

SHANGHAI RADISH FILLING

4 cups shredded Daikon Radish

½ cup chopped Salty Ham or
rehydrated Shitake Mushrooms

4 Green Onions, trimmed
and sliced thin

2 Tablespoons Vegetable Oil

1 teaspoon Salt

1 teaspoon Sugar

Heat oil in a frying pan and add in the Green Onion. Cook until you can smell their fragrance. Then add in the Daikon Radish and the Ham or Shitake Mushroom pieces. Cook until the Radish gets soft and then season with Salt, Sugar and White Pepper. Cool before using as a filling.

NOTE: For Vegan Egg Replacement, we use 2 Tablespoons Flax Seed Meal mixed with 2 Tablespoons of Water

On any Dim Sum Cart around the world, you will see golden brown Sticky Rice Balls studded with Sesame Seeds. Inside you will usually find a filling made from Sweetened Red Bean Paste. We like to make our own Red Bean Paste, but you can easily buy premade Red Bean Paste Filling at any Asian grocery store. You could also get creative and fill them instead with Coconut and Brown Sugar or use our recipe for Pineapple filling or stuff them with the Char Siu filling. Like all fried foods, these Sesame Rice Balls are best when freshly made, but you can reheat them in the oven if you have any left over.

Sesame Rice Balls

STICKY RICE DOUGH

2 cups Sticky Rice Flour
+ ⅓ cup more for rolling out

1 teaspoon Baking Powder

1 teaspoon Salt

2 teaspoons Sugar

1 cup Boiling Water

½ cup of Sesame Seeds

Vegetable Oil for frying

In a large bowl, mix the Sticky Rice Flour with the Baking Powder, Salt and Sugar. Pour in the boiling water and stir quickly with a spoon. Pres into a ball and put on a Rice Flour dusted cutting board. Roll out and cut into 3½-inch circles.

Pour the Sesame Seeds into a shallow bowl. Press each dough Circle into the Sesame Seeds. Then turn it seed side down and fill with 1 Tablespoon of the filling. Bring up the sides and pinch to form a ball.

Heat 3–4 cups of Oil in a deep fryer or a wok. When the Oil is hot, drop in several Sesame Balls. Fry until they are golden brown. Remove to a paper towel covered plate to drain and repeat until all the Sesame Balls are cooked. Serve immediately or refrigerate and reheat in a 300°F oven until hot.

RED BEAN PASTE FILLING

½ cup Chinese Red Beans
(small Azuki Beans)

Water for Soaking

¼ cup Sugar

1 Tablespoon of Vegetable
Oil, Coconut Oil or Lard

a pinch of Salt

Wash the Red Beans and soak them in water, covering them by 2 inches.
Soak overnight. Drain and place in a pot. Add 2 cups of Water and bring to
a boil. Reduce heat and simmer. Cook the Beans for one hour or until they
are very soft. Drain the Beans, reserving the cooking liquid. Add the Sugar
and the Oil (or Coconut Oil or Lard) to the Beans and stir until combined.
Smash the Beans with a Potato Masher. Add some Water back in until the
consistency is like paste. If desired, you can puree the Bean Paste in a food
processor or blender.

If you prefer a very smooth paste, press the Red Bean Mixture through
a fine mesh metal strainer, pushing the Paste through with the back of a
large spoon into a bowl to remove the skins. Then put the Paste back in the
pan and add in the Sugar, Salt and Oil and cook until the Red Bean Paste
becomes sticky and thick.

Cool and refrigerate the Red Bean Paste
until ready to use.

CHAPTER 8

Savory Bites

Lotus Root Chips are beautiful and taste a bit like fried Potatoes. We make them often and we like to bake them. You could also deep-fry these Chips, but this version is much easier and we think healthier too. Just be sure to cook them on parchment paper so they don't stick to the pan. You can also substitute Daikon Radish if you can't find Lotus Root. We usually have to make a double and sometimes a triple batch, as we all love these Lotus Root Chips so much!

Baked Lotus Root or Daikon Radish Chips

1 pound of Lotus Root or Daikon Radish, ends cut off and peeled
3 Tablespoons Vegetable Oil
¼ teaspoon Salt or Chinese Seasoned Salt

Heat the oven to 375°F. Line a Baking Pan with Parchment Paper. Slice the Lotus Root tor Daikon Radish very thin (about ¼ inch thick) and place in a bowl with the Oil. Then toss to coat. Place the Lotus Root or Daikon Radish Slices onto the Baking Pan. Sprinkle with Salt and place in the oven. Cook for 15 minutes or more until they are lightly golden brown.

Small Potatoes spiced with Cumin are a popular street food in Xi'an. My Daughter-in-Law told us about them so we decided to make some. We all loved them so much, that we now make them often. I have to use less Chili Powder on mine, but everyone else likes lots of Chili on their serving.

Xi'an Spiced Potatoes

12 small new Potatoes, washed

2 Tablespoons Sichuan Chili Oil or Vegetable Oil

3 Garlic cloves, minced

1–2 Tablespoons Korean or Sichuan Chili Powder

2 teaspoons ground Cumin

1 teaspoon Salt

1 teaspoon Sugar

About 3 Tablespoons Green Onion tops, cut into small pieces

Place Potatoes in a pot and cover with water. Bring to a boil and reduce heat to a simmer. Cook for 20 minutes. Drain.

Then heat the Oil in a wok until the oil shimmers. Add the Garlic and cook until you smell the fragrance. Add in the Potatoes and toss to coat and then cook until the Potatoes start to crisp. Then, sprinkle in the Chili Powder, Cumin, Salt and Sugar. Toss to combine and pour onto a serving plate and sprinkle with Green Onions.

Radish Cake is a savory Dim Sum delight! It is often called Turnip Cake, but it is actually made from lots of grated Daikon Radish along with Green Onions and Shitake Mushrooms. It often contains Chinese Sausage, but we can't find any without Red Food Coloring or Wheat, so we make our family's Radish Cake with either some homemade Chinese Bacon that incorporates the same flavors or cut up some Salty Ham to add in and we often leave the meat out altogether. Radish Cake is steamed, then cut into slices and pan-fried. It's so much tastier than it sounds and it's something we always make for Chinese New Year, as it is considered a good luck food.

Radish Cake

5 cups peeled and shredded Daikon Radish (about 2 pounds)

2 Tablespoons Oil

1 large Shallot minced

¼ cup Chicken or Vegetable Broth

2 cups Rice Flour

4 Green Onions, trimmed and cut into small pieces (about 1 cup)

6–8 dried Shitake Mushrooms

2 teaspoons Salt

½ teaspoon Sugar

⅓ cup of Cilantro Leaves for serving

OPTIONAL

1 cup Chinese Bacon Bits or Salty Ham cut into small pieces

Soak the Shitake Mushrooms in boiling water to cover until they are completely softened and cool, about 30 minutes. Then cut off the stem and cut into small pieces—it should be close to 1 cup.

Heat a frying pan and add in the Oil. Add in the Shallot and cook until you can smell the fragrance. Then add in the Daikon Radish with the Salt, Sugar and Broth. Cook over low heat with a lid on for 20 minutes, stirring occasionally.

Then add in the Green Onions and Mushroom pieces and the Chinese Bacon or bits of Ham, if using. Then add in the Rice Flour and mix thoroughly. If you like a softer Radish Cake, add an additional 2 Tablespoons of Broth.

Pour into an oiled 8 or 9-inch square pan and pat down the top to make it smooth. Cover with aluminum foil and place in a steamer rack in a steamer pot or in a bamboo steamer rack over a wok, filled with water. Bring the Water to a boil, then turn the heat down and steam for 1 hour. Take the Radish Cake out and let cool completely.

Remove the Radish Cake from the pan and slice into ¼ inch¼ x 2-inch slices. Heat a frying pan with 1 Tablespoon of Oil and add the Radish Cake slices. Cook until they are browned on one side and then turn over to brown the other side. Remove to a plate. Add more Oil if necessary, for each batch and continue to cook until all slices are browned. Drizzle with the Sauce (below).

FOR SAUCE: Mix ¼ cup of Sweet Tamari with ¼ cup of Mushroom Tamari and drizzle over the slices of Radish Cake. Sprinkle with Cilantro to serve.

These Tofu Balls are much more than a substitute for Meatballs. They are definitely delicious in their own right. They are juicy on the inside and crisp on the outside. We sometimes change things up and add some Curry Powder for a different taste. These Fried Tofu and Mushroom Balls are wonderful dipped into any number of dipping sauces.

Fried Tofu and Mushroom Balls

1 block of Medium or
Firm Tofu, pressed

3 Tablespoons Mushroom Tamari,
Tamari or GF Soy Sauce

1½ Tablespoons toasted
Sesame Oil

½ teaspoon Salt

⅓ cup finely minced Green Onion

6 dried Shitake Mushrooms

¾ cup Potato Starch

OPTIONAL

1 Tablespoon Curry Powder

Oil for deep-frying

Rehydrate the Mushrooms in boiling water and soak until cool. Slice off the stem and then cut into slivers and then mince.

Crumble the Tofu into a mixing bowl and then mash with a fork. Add in the Mushroom Tamari, Sesame Oil and Salt along with the Green Onions and Shitake Mushrooms. Mix well. Form into walnut sized balls and place on a plate.

Heat Oil in a wok or deep fryer. Put the Potato Starch on a plate and coat each Tofu Ball thoroughly. Return to the plate. Drop a few Tofu Balls at a time in the hot Oil and cook until they are golden brown. Drain on a paper towel covered plate. Continue until all the Tofu Balls are fried. Serve immediately with the Dipping Sauce of your choice. To reheat, place under the broiler until re-crisped.

This is a recipe Stephen created one afternoon when we found that we needed to use up some Egg Tofu that I had bought. Egg Tofu comes in a tube and is made from Eggs and Soy Milk. So, we sliced it and pan-fried it. Then we had to think of what to put on top. Stephen whipped up some Mapo Tofu without the Tofu and also some Shitake Mushrooms, cooked in the style of Eel. Tofu Sliders were born and they are a Keto delight as Tofu is a substitute for buns. You can use Firm Tofu instead, cut into squares with the Mushroom Sliders if you are Vegan. If you don't want to use Tofu, these toppings are also delicious on baked slices of Chinese or Japanese Eggplant.

Tofu Sliders

FOR THE TOFU

2 packages Egg Tofu, removed from the package and sliced into ½–¾-inch slices or 1 package of Firm Tofu cut into 4 squares and cut lengthwise in half
2 Tablespoons Vegetable Oil

Heat a non-stick frying pan and add in the Oil. Carefully put in the Tofu pieces and pan fry until browned and then turn over carefully to brown the other side. Remove to a plate and spoon on the topping of your choice.

MAPO TOFU TOPPING

⅓–½ pound of ground Pork or Chicken

3 Green Onions cut into small pieces – separate white part from the green part

1 large Garlic Clove minced

¼ x 1-inch slice of Ginger, peeled and minced finely

3 Tablespoons Tamari or GF Soy Sauce

1 Tablespoon Rice Wine

2 teaspoons Hoisin Sauce

2 teaspoons Chili Garlic Sauce

1 teaspoon toasted Sesame Oil

3 Tablespoons Vegetable Oil

¼ cup Chicken Broth

1 Tablespoon Cornstarch mixed with enough water to make a slurry

OPTIONAL

a pinch of ground Sichuan Pepper Salt

Place ground Pork or Chicken in a small bowl. Add 1 Tablespoon of Tamari along with the Rice Wine and the Hoisin Sauce. Mix in thoroughly and put aside to marinate for a few minutes.

Mix together the Chicken Broth, remaining Tamari and Chili Paste in a small bowl. Put aside.

Pour the Oil into a heated frying pan or wok and add in the white part of the Green Onions with the Ginger and Garlic. Cook for a few minutes until you can smell the fragrance. Add in ground Pork or Chicken and cook until it is no longer pink. Add in the Chicken Broth mixture and boil for a few more minutes. Add in Cornstarch and Sesame Oil and stir to thicken. Then add in green part of Green Onions and Szechuan Pepper Salt, if using. Spoon onto the pan-fried Egg Tofu or Tofu Squares and sprinkle with reserved Green Onions.

SHITAKE MUSHROOM TOPPING

7 ounces of dried Shitake Mushrooms,
6 cups boiling Water
1 Tablespoon Vegetable Oil
2 Green Onions, white and green part separated, cut into small pieces
½ x 1-inch piece of Ginger, grated

¼ cup Tamari
2 Tablespoons Rice Wine
1 Tablespoon Sugar
¼ teaspoon toasted Sesame Oil
a pinch of White Pepper
1 teaspoon Cornstarch mixed with 2 teaspoons of Water

In a small bowl, mix together the Tamari, Rice Wine, Sugar, Sesame Oil and White Pepper.

Soak the Shitake Mushrooms in the boiling water for about 30 minutes or until completely softened. Cut off the stem end and then dice.

Heat a frying pan and add in the Oil. Then add in the white part of the Green Onions and Ginger. Cook until you smell the fragrance. Then add in the prepared Mushrooms or Eggplant and cook until they are hot. Then add in the Tamari mixture and cook until bubbling. Then add in the Cornstarch and cook until thickened. Spoon onto the Tofu pieces and sprinkle with the remaining Green Onions.

EGGPLANT SLIDERS OPTION

Heat the oven to 375°F.

Trim the ends of 3 Chinese or Japanese Eggplants and cut into ¾-inch wide slices. Place them onto an oiled baking sheet and drizzle with an additional 2–3 Tablespoons of Oil. Cook for 15 minutes, turn over and cook for an additional 10 minutes or until lightly browned, but not too soft. Remove from oven and top with either of the above toppings.

At most Dim Sum restaurants, you can find Steamed Beef Meatballs flavored with dried Mandarin Orange Peel, Cilantro or Green Onions with Water Chestnuts added for some crunchy texture. These Meatballs are traditionally cooked and served in individual bowls on top of small sheets of Tofu Skin to collect the sauce it creates. We make them with both Cilantro and Green Onions and we often cook them in a pie pan lined with Napa Cabbage leaves if we don't have any Tofu Skins on hand. We also sometimes broil them. They are traditionally served with Worcestershire Sauce in Dim Sum restaurants, although we serve them with our own Meatball Dipping Sauce or Green Onion and Ginger Relish.

Steamed Beef Meatballs

1 pound ground Beef

1 8-oz can of Water Chestnuts, drained

3 Tablespoons Tamari or GF Soy Sauce

2 Tablespoons Rice Wine

½ teaspoon Salt

1 Egg, lightly beaten

2 Tablespoons minced Cilantro Leaves

2 slender Green Onions, minced

2 pieces (about 1-inch inch) of dried Mandarin Orange Peel, soaked in boiling water

Tofu Skins or Napa Cabbage

FOR COOKING: 1 or 2 large Sheets of Tofu Skins, rehydrated in water and cut into pieces big enough to fit in the bottom of whatever size bowls you are using, or use pieces of Napa Cabbage.

Mince the Water Chestnuts and the Orange Peel very fine and put into a mixing bowl. Then add the Beef, Tamari, Rice Wine, Egg, Cilantro, Green Onions and Water Chestnuts and mix together thoroughly with your hands. Make into Meatballs about the size of a Walnut.

Heat water in a steamer pot or in a wok with a bamboo steamer on top. Place pieces of Tofu Skin or Napa Cabbage in the bowls you are using and top with the Meatballs. Steam for 10 minutes to cook.

Makes about 26

We love Meatballs of all kinds and our family version incorporates either Ground Pork, which is traditional, or ground Chicken along with minced Green Onions, Shitake Mushrooms and Water Chestnuts. Deep-frying these Meatballs makes them the most attractive, as they keep their round shape and cook more evenly. But you can also pan-fry them, or broil them, if you prefer.

We usually serve them with several different Dipping Sauces, especially at parties and they are wonderful tossed in Sweet and Sour Sauce or General Tso's Sauce. We've also included a Glaze that can be used to coat them if you want to serve them as a main dish. They are delicious any way you make them!

Lowe Family Pork or Chicken Meatballs

1 pound of ground Pork or Chicken

½ cup (about 5) dried
Shitake Mushrooms

½ cup Water Chestnuts
(from a can), drained and minced

3 Green Onions, trimmed
and minced finely

2 Tablespoons Tamari
or GF Soy Sauce

2 Tablespoons Rice Wine

1 Egg White

a pinch of White Pepper

OPTIONAL

½ teaspoon grated Ginger

Vegetable Oil for frying

Soak the Shitake Mushrooms in boiling water until soft. Then cut them in half, cut out the hard stem and mince them.

Mix together the ground Pork or Chicken with the Shitake Mushrooms, Green Onions, Tamari, Rice Wine, Egg White and Ginger, if using. Form into small Meatballs.

Makes about 24

TO BROIL: place the Meatballs on an oiled baking sheet. Place under the broiler for 10 minutes. Brush with glaze if desired and cook for 2–3 minutes more.

TO DEEP FRY: heat 3–4 cups Vegetable Oil in a deep fryer or a wok. Cook until the Meatballs become a deep golden brown, about 2½–3 minutes.

TO PAN FRY: heat 2 Tablespoons of Vegetable Oil in a frying pan and put in the Meatballs. Cook on both sides until golden brown, about 5 minutes per side.

GLAZE

2 Tablespoons low Sodium Tamari or GF Soy Sauce

2 Tablespoons Rice Wine

2 Tablespoons Sugar

1 Tablespoon Rice Vinegar

a few drops of Sesame Oil

If you take the Meatballs from the recipe above and roll them in soaked Sticky Rice and steam them, you get Pearl Balls. This poetic name implies that Rice becomes shiny and iridescent and glistens like Pearls. The other nickname is Porcupine Balls, as the coating of Rice sticks out from the meatball inside. Whatever you call them, these delightful rice-covered Meatballs are often served for special occasions. We like to make the Pearl Balls on the small side so that you can pop them into your mouth with only one or two bites!

Steamed Pearl Balls

1 recipe of Meatballs
1 cup Short Grain White Rice
4 Napa Cabbage leaves

Soak the Rice in a bowl with warm water to cover for at least 8 hours, preferably overnight.

Place the Napa Cabbage leaves on two plates that fit into a bamboo steamer. Drain the Rice and spread onto another baking sheet. Roll each Meatball in the Rice and place it on the plate. Repeat until all the Pearl Balls are made. Put both plates inside the two layers of the bamboo steamer.

Put water in the bottom of the wok to a depth of at least 4 inches and heat to boiling. Place the bamboo steamer on top of the wok and steam for 20–25 minutes. Serve with any of the Dumpling Dipping Sauces.

My grandfather used to cook what he called Peking Fried Chicken and it was a family favorite for all generations. We still make Fried Chicken his way and Tofu too. You have a choice of tossing any of the Sauces with the Fried Chicken or Tofu or serving them as dipping sauces instead.

We have also included the Taiwanese version of Popcorn Chicken that is served at their famous Night Market. The unique flavor of this dish comes from the addition of fried Basil Leaves.

Chinese Fried Chicken or Tofu

1 pound boneless, skinless Chicken Thighs (about 4) or Breasts (about 2 halves) cut into chunks or Chicken Tenders or Chicken Wings, or Firm Tofu, cut in cubes

¼ cup Tamari or GF Soy Sauce

¼ cup Rice Wine

1 teaspoon Sugar

1½-inch chunk of fresh Ginger, sliced (no need to peel)

½ cup of Cornstarch

4 cups of Vegetable Oil for frying

FOR SERVING

2–3 Green Onion tops sliced very thin

1 Tablespoons Sesame Seeds

In a large mixing bowl, stir the Tamari, Rice Wine and Sugar together. Add the Ginger and Chicken or Tofu and toss to combine. Marinate for at least 20 minutes up to 24 hours in the refrigerator.

When ready to fry, heat the oil in a deep fryer or wok until it is hot.

Drain off most of the marinade, reserving a few Tablespoons of marinade on the bottom of the bowl. Sprinkle on the Cornstarch. Toss the Chicken or Tofu pieces until they are coated in the sticky Cornstarch mixture.

Cook the Chicken or Tofu pieces until deep golden brown and remove with a wire mesh strainer or slotted spoon. When each batch is done, place on paper towel lined plate until all are done.

Sprinkle with Green Onion tops and Sesame Seeds. Toss with the sauce of your choice or serve the sauce on the side as a dip.

Taiwanese Popcorn Chicken or Tofu Variation:

Use bite-sized pieces of Chicken or Tofu and dredge in 1 cup of Sweet Potato Starch or Potato Starch. Fry as directed above. When done, quickly fry 1 cup of Thai Basil leaves in the still-hot Oil. Mix the Basil, ¼ teaspoon Salt or Sichuan Pepper Salt and a large pinch of White Pepper and sprinkle over the Chicken, tossing to coat.

Apricot Chili Sauce was one of the first sauces I learned to make as a child. Back then, I wanted something sweet to dip my fried Wontons into and my Mom made this sauce for me. Like all overseas Chinese, she adapted to what she had on hand and my father loved Apricot Jam on toast. So, we always had some in the fridge and she used it to make a variation of the more traditional Plum Sauce. This is a favorite sauce in our family and a few years back we had the great idea of using it with broiled Chicken Wings and we were completely smitten. Chicken Wings coated with this sticky, sweet and as spicy Apricot Sauce are wonderful! Of course, you can cook these Chicken Wings on the grill if you prefer before you add the Sauce. This is a very sticky sauce, so be sure to have plenty of napkins on hand for wiping off your fingers!

Apricot Chili Chicken Wings

3 pounds of Chicken Wings, middle section if possible or split at the joints with the wing tip removed

1 teaspoon Salt

½ teaspoon Pepper

¾–1 cup Apricot Jam or Preserves (preferably low in Sugar)

3 Tablespoons Tamari or GF Soy Sauce + 1 Tbsp more if Jam is very sweet

2 Tablespoons Rice Vinegar

1 teaspoon or more Chili Garlic Sauce or Sriracha

1 Tablespoon Vegetable Oil

1 Green Onion, trimmed and cut into small pieces

½ teaspoon grated Ginger

1–2 Garlic cloves, minced

2 Tablespoons Chicken Broth or Water

In a bowl, mix together the Apricot, Jam, Tamari, Rice Vinegar and Chili Garlic Sauce. Taste and adjust seasoning, adding more Tamari or Chili Garlic Sauce, as desired.

In a small frying pan, heat the Oil and add in the Green Onions, Ginger and Garlic. Cook until you can smell their fragrance strongly. Then add in the sauce mixture. Bring to a boil and remove from heat.

Turn the oven on to broil. Line 2 large rimmed baking sheets with foil (unless you don't mind scrubbing the baking sheets later). Arrange the Wings in a single layer on each of the prepared baking sheets. Cook for 10 minutes or until the skin is browned. Turn the Wings over and broil for an additional 10 minutes or until that side is browned. Repeat with the remaining Wings, but cook for 12 minutes. When the second batch is done, return the first batch to the oven and cook for an additional 2–4 minutes or until they are hot.

Then place all the Chicken Wings in a large serving bowl and pour the sauce over. Toss thoroughly to coat the Wings evenly.

If you like Ribs, you know that there is something so satisfying about gnawing flavorful meat off bones and this recipe delivers Ribs with a lot of flavor. The Spareribs are marinated in a Hot Hoisin Barbecue Sauce before being cooked low and slow in the oven and it's so worth the wait!

Hot Hoisin Barbecued Spareribs

2 pounds of Pork Spareribs, cut in half by the Butcher

⅓ cup Gluten Free Hoisin Sauce

½ cup Tamari or GF Soy Sauce

¼ cup Rice Wine

½ Tablespoon–2 Tablespoons Chili Garlic Sauce or Sriracha

⅓ cup Brown Sugar

2 large Garlic cloves. minced fine

Place all of the sauce ingredients in a small pot and stir until thoroughly mixed. Heat over low heat until the Sugar is dissolved. Then just bring to a boil. Remove from heat.

Reserve half of the Hot Hoisin Barbecue Sauce and place in the refrigerator. Pour the other half of the Sauce into a large sealing plastic bag. Add the Spareribs and marinate for 2–3 hours or overnight in the refrigerator. The longer you marinate the Spareribs before you cook them, the better they taste.

Preheat the oven to 250°F. Place a large sheet of aluminum foil in a large baking dish horizontally. Place two other sheets of aluminum foil going the other direction. Pull up the sides and put in the Spareribs and the marinade. Bake in the oven for 2 hours.

Take the reserved sauce out of the refrigerator. Pour into a small saucepan. Heat until the sauce is warm.

Remove the Spareribs from the oven, open the foil and brush the Spareribs with the basting sauce. Turn the oven up to 350°F and place the pan back in the oven, cooking for an additional 45 minutes, basting the Spareribs every 15 minutes. Remove from the oven and cut into individual Ribs with kitchen scissors or a sharp boning knife. Place the Ribs on a large platter to serve.

This dish is most often found on Dim Sum Carts where you get only a few small pieces and I always wanted more. So, here's how you make these wonderful Savory Spareribs at home, steamed the traditional way with an option to use the Pressure Cooker, which we think makes them more tender. The timing is dependent on the kind of Pressure Cooker you have. I have an old stove top one and it takes longer, whereas Stephen has a newer electric one and the Ribs cook much faster in it! A lot of people use jarred Black Bean Sauce instead of sourcing them at an Asian market, but they can now be bought online. And it's so much better when you use the actual Salted Black Beans in this homemade sauce. It gives these Ribs a special savory flavor that is hard to describe, but is absolutely delicious!

Steamed Black Bean Spareribs

2 pounds Pork Spareribs cut into 1-inch pieces by the butcher

2 Tablespoons Vegetable Oil

4 cloves Garlic, minced fine

1 heaping Tablespoon of Ginger, peeled and minced or grated

¼ cup salted Black Beans, mashed with a fork

2 teaspoons Sugar

1 teaspoon Salt

¼ cup Rice Wine

4 teaspoons Tamari or GF Soy Sauce

⅓ cup Chicken Broth or Water

½ teaspoon toasted Sesame Oil

1 Tablespoon Cornstarch

FOR GARNISH

1 Green Onion, green part only, cut into small pieces or some Cilantro Leaves

In a small bowl, mix together the Chicken Broth, Sesame Oil and Cornstarch

Put Oil in a frying pan and add Garlic, Ginger and Black Beans and cook until you can smell the fragrance. Then add in the Sugar, Rice Wine and Tamari. Stir to mix well and bring to a boil. Then add in the Chicken Broth and Cornstarch and cook until slightly thickened.

Place the Spareribs in a large sealing plastic bag and pour in the Sauce, Seal the bag and shake to coat them thoroughly. Let the Spareribs marinate for at least 30 minutes or overnight in the refrigerator.

STEAMER METHOD

When ready to cook, place the Ribs in a bowl in a bamboo steamer over a wok full of boiling water or in a steamer pot. Cook on medium high for about 15 minutes. Turn the Spareribs over and cook for another 15 minutes. Sprinkle with Green Onion pieces or Cilantro leaves to serve.

PRESSURE COOKER METHOD

Put the Spareribs and marinating liquid into a Pressure Cooker. Seal and cook for 20 minutes. Check the Ribs, and if the meat is not falling-off-the-bone tender, cook for an additional 5–10 minutes. Then remove the Ribs and pour into a bowl. Sprinkle with Green Onions pieces or Cilantro leaves to serve.

This is a classic Dim Sum dish where Black Pepper is the featured flavor. The Beef Short Ribs are steamed and become tender and delicious. Although they are usually served in individual small bowls, this recipe makes enough for dinner if you add several side dishes.

Cantonese Steamed Black Pepper Short Ribs

1 pound of Beef Short Ribs, cut into bite size pieces following the bones on the top

1 Onion, trimmed and thinly sliced

1 Tablespoon Oil

2 cloves Garlic, minced

2 Tablespoons Rice Wine

1 Tablespoon Tamari or GF Soy Sauce

1 Tablespoons Mushroom Tamari

1 teaspoon Sugar

¼ teaspoon fresh ground Black Pepper

1 Tablespoon Cornstarch

½ Tablespoon toasted Sesame Oil

Marinate the Beef Short Ribs in the Garlic, Sugar, Rice Wine and Tamari.

When ready to cook, add the Black Pepper, Sesame Oil and then the Cornstarch. Mix well.

Sauté the Onions in a small frying pan with the Oil. Cook until they are just starting to brown. Put the Onions on the bottom of a bowl that fits inside a bamboo steamer. Put the Marinated Beef on top and place in the steamer over boiling water. Cook for 20 minutes, turn the Ribs over and cook for an additional 10 minutes. Remove and serve hot.

CHAPTER 9
Wraps & Rolls

Rou Ji Mao Sandwiches

These famous sandwiches are often called Chinese Hamburgers, although they are really more like Sloppy Joes. They are a specialty from the Shaanxi region of China and are a very popular street food there and throughout Northern China. The crusty flatbread is usually stuffed with chopped Red Braised Pork Belly and topped with Cilantro or Pickled Mustard Greens and are usually drizzled with lots of Chili Oil. We like to stuff them with a variety of fillings and use different sauces for each. We often serve them with the Xi'an Cilantro, Celery and Onion Salad or top them with lots of Tamari Ginger Cucumbers that we use as Pickles. The traditional Bai Ji Mao Flatbreads were oven-baked, but most street vendors pan-fry them these days. We've given you a baked version, although you could certainly cook them on the stove. These Buns are dense and crisp and a bit like Cracker Bread. You can easily substitute Gluten Free English Muffins, but be sure to toast them. Rou Ji Mao Sandwiches are delicious!

Bai Ji Mao Flatbread

2 cups Gluten-Free Flour Blend
(*See recipe on page 27*)

1 teaspoons Salt

1 teaspoon Baking Powder

¾ cup Boiling Water

2 Tablespoons Vegetable Oil

¼ cup Warm Water

2 teaspoons Active Dry Yeast

1 teaspoon Sugar

Egg Wash: 1 Egg lightly beaten

2 Tablespoons Sesame Seeds

In a measuring cup, mix together the warm Water, Yeast and Sugar. Let the mixture proof until the Yeast bubbles.

Put the Gluten-Free Flour Blend in a mixing bowl and add in the Baking Powder and Salt. Mix to combine. Then add in the Oil and Boiling Water. Mix thoroughly. Then add in the Yeast mixture until thoroughly incorporated. Shape the dough into a ball. Cover the bowl with plastic wrap and let rise for about one hour.

Then cut the dough into 5 pieces and pat out each piece to about 4 inches.

Heat oven to 350°F. Brush the tops with an Egg Wash and sprinkle with Sesame Seeds. Bake for 25–30 minutes or until golden brown.

To Stuff: Split the Rolls carefully with a bread knife. Stuff with the filling of your choice, sprinkle with chopped Cilantro leaves and Chili Oil and/or Tamari Ginger Cucumber Pickles.

Makes 4

One of the foods I missed most when I became Gluten-Free was Green Onion Pancakes. I loved their crispy, chewy texture with savory Green Onion pieces speckling the dough. It was a challenge to create Green Onion Pancakes without wheat, but we finally succeeded in creating two versions! One uses a Gluten-Free Flour Blend that browns beautifully. We like to eat these dipped into the Lowe Family Dumping Sauce, Chili Garlic Sauce, Green Onion and Ginger Relish or the Cilantro and Green Chili Relish. The other version uses Cassava Flour that makes a chewier Green Onion Pancake and we like it best as a wrapper since they bend easily. It is also a grain-free option. We think that the secret to making Green Onion Pancakes is to flavor the cooking oil with Green Onion Oil and the crispy Green Onion bits left over make a wonderful garnish for many dishes.

Green Onion Pancakes

2 cups Gluten-Free Flour Blend
(See recipe on page 27)
or Cassava Flour
1 teaspoon fine Sea Salt
1 teaspoon Baking Powder
¼ cup toasted Sesame Oil

1 cup Boiling Water
⅓ cup Vegetable Oil for Cooking
6 Green Onions, trimmed – white
and green parts separated,
cut into small pieces
½ teaspoon coarse Sea
Salt for garnish

In a small frying pan, heat the Vegetable Oil and add in the white part of the Green Onions. Cook until the Green Onion pieces start to brown. Remove from heat and drain off the Oil, reserving the cooked Green Onion pieces for garnish.

In a large mixing bowl, mix together the Gluten-Free Flour Blend or Cassava Flour, Baking Powder and fine Sea Salt. Add in the Green Onions. Then add in Boiling Water and the Sesame Oil. Stir until combined. If it is too dry, add an additional 1 Tablespoon of Water at a time, until the dough comes together. Or if the dough is too soft, add an additional 1 Tablespoon of Flour.

Divide the dough into 4 pieces for large Pancakes or 6 pieces for smaller Pancakes. Make each piece into a ball and press between two pieces of Parchment Paper or Wax Paper to create Pancakes about ⅓-inch thick. Repeat with the remaining dough.

Heat a 12-inch frying pan and add 1 Tablespoon of the Green Onion Oil. Place one or two of the Green Onion Pancakes in the pan and cook until golden brown, turn and cook on the other side until it is browned. Remove to a plate and sprinkle with a little coarse Sea Salt. Repeat until all the Green Onion Pancakes are cooked. Serve with the dipping sauce of your choice.

Makes 4

Green Onion Pancake Wraps

Use the recipe for Green Onion Pancakes using Cassava Flour. When the Green Onion Pancakes are done, fold them in half and stuff with either Spiced Sliced Beef, Char Siu Pork, Chicken or Tofu, Tamari Mushrooms or Baked Marinated Tofu Slices. Sprinkle with Cilantro and drizzle with the sauce of your choice.

When my Mother used to have dinner parties, she would often make a big tray of cold, sliced Chinese meats. It was very exotic for our American guests, but perfectly normal for us, as my Grandfather made these same meats often. One of my favorites was Spiced Sliced Beef Shanks that are cooked long and slow in a deeply seasoned broth making the meat soft, savory and delicious. When the Beef Shank is done, save the full-flavored broth and make it into a sauce or use it as a base for noodle soup with some of the Beef Shank chopped up and added in. Be sure to refrigerate the Shanks before you slice them as they are much easier to slice when cold. These Spiced Beef Slices are great as part of a meat platter and we love to use them as a delicious filling for Green Onion Pancake Wraps or chopped up for Rou Jia Mo Sandwiches.

Spiced Sliced Beef

5 Green Onions, cut in half

4–6 large cloves of Garlic, peeled

2 Star Anise pods

3 Bay Leaves

a 2-inch piece of Ginger peeled and sliced into 3 pieces

1 stick of Cinnamon

4 whole dried Red Chiles

1 heaping Tablespoon Sichuan Peppercorns

1 large Onion, peeled and cut into eight pieces

1 large Carrot, peeled and cut into 4 pieces

1 bunch of Cilantro, washed and bottom root end cut off

4 Tablespoons Rock Sugar

1 cup Rice Wine

1 cup Low Sodium Tamari or GF Soy Sauce

1 teaspoon White Pepper

8 cups Water

2 teaspoons Salt

1 Black Cardamom Pod

FOR SERVING

¼ cup Cilantro Leaves and ¼ cup Green Onion pieces

Place Beef Shanks in a pot and barely cover with cold water. Bring to a boil and then remove from heat. Take out the Beef Shank and set aside. Then dump out the water and foam and clean out the pot. Place the Beef Shanks back in the pot and add in 8 cups of Water and all of the seasonings and vegetables. Return to a boil, cover, and reduce heat to a simmer. Cook the Beef Shanks for 3 hours, or until the they can be pierced easily with a fork.

Remove the Beef Shanks and place in a container. Strain the Broth, reserving about 1 cup and add that to the Beef Shanks and refrigerate until cold. Freeze the remaining Broth to use later as a soup base or use as a Master Sauce to make this recipe again. When ready to use, take the Beef Shanks out and slice thinly.

TO MAKE THE SAUCE

Pour the gelatinized broth left in the container into a small pot. Heat until warm. Taste and add a little Salt, if desired. Mix 2 teaspoons of Cornstarch with 1 Tablespoon of Water and add to the Sauce. Bring to a boil and reduce to a simmer, stirring until thickened. Use this sauce to drizzle over the Beef, if serving as part of a meat platter or when making Green Onion Pancake Wraps.

Char Siu Pork can be seen hanging in the windows of Chinese Delis all over the world and it is delicious. Unfortunately for those of us with allergies, the commercial marinades are usually a mixture of Soy Sauce, Hoisin Sauce and Rice Wine that all contain Wheat and they use Red Food Coloring too.

This recipe creates the same wonderful Char Siu Pork without any Wheat or Red Food Coloring. If you want to make the meat look redder, you can use Beet Powder, although it will change the taste and I don't think it looks any better. This marinade also works well with Chicken Thighs or Tofu. Make sure you marinate your Pork, Chicken or Tofu for an adequate amount of time, as you want it to absorb the sauce thoroughly before cooking. We recommend serving Char Siu stuffed into Bai Ji Mo Flatbreads or into Green Onion Pancakes with a drizzle of some of the sauce on top. Char Siu is also really good dipped into some Chinese Hot Mustard.

Char Siu – Chinese Barbecued Pork/Chicken/Tofu

2 1/2 pounds of Pork Butt cut into 4 long pieces or a Pork Tenderloin

or 2 pounds of boneless Chicken Thighs or 2 packages Firm Tofu, drained

3 cloves of Garlic, minced

½ cup Gluten Free Hoisin Sauce

3 Tablespoons Rice Wine

2 Tablespoons Golden Syrup

2 Tablespoons Tamari or GF Soy Sauce

2 Tablespoons Ketchup

1 Tablespoon Rice Vinegar

1 teaspoon toasted Sesame Oil

OPTIONAL

1 teaspoon Beet Powder

FOR SERVING

1–2 Tablespoons Sesame Seeds

In a small frying pan, heat all the sauce ingredients until blended and warm. Place the Pork, Chicken or Tofu in a foil-covered baking dish and pour the sauce over. Turn several times and cover with plastic wrap and place in the refrigerator for 4 hours up to overnight, turning at least once. When you are ready to cook, heat the oven to 375°F.

Pour off the marinade and put in a small frying pan and cook until boiling. Reserve and use for basting and serving.*

Place the Pork or Chicken in the oven and cook for 30 minutes. Then turn over, baste and cook for another 30 minutes.

If using Pork Tenderloin or Tofu, you can also cook at 400°F for 25 minutes for Tofu or 40 minutes for Pork Tenderloin.

Then turn on the broiler and cook each side for 2–3 minutes or until the Meat or Tofu starts to char slightly. Watch carefully so that it doesn't burn. Take the Meat or Tofu out of the oven and let it cool for 10 minutes on a serving platter. Slice and sprinkle with the Sesame Seeds.

*Or make double the marinade and reserve half in the refrigerator for serving. Heat before using as a sauce.

Red Cooked Pork Belly is a classic Chinese dish, where calling it red is a fanciful way of describing the rich brown color of the Pork Belly after it has cooked for several hours in a Soy Sauce based sauce. This is my family's recipe and we use it in this cookbook as a filling for Rou Jia Mo Sandwiches, where it is minced and piled onto Bai Ji Mo flatbreads. Pork Belly takes a long time to cook, but it's worth it, as it results in meat that is rich and savory. It's actually best if you cook Pork Belly a day before to let the flavors meld and then you can also skim off the fat before you reheat it. The leftover sauce should be saved (frozen) and reused later. Spareribs, Chicken Thighs, Chicken Wings or Tofu can all easily be substituted, but all of these will take less time to cook. And of course, you can easily use a pressure cooker to shorten the cooking time. We serve Pork Belly cooked like this every Chinese New Year.

Red Cooked Pork Belly/Chicken/Tofu

2 pounds of Pork Belly, cut into chunks or Spareribs, Chicken Thighs, Chicken Wings or Tofu

2 cups Water

2 cups Chicken or Vegetable Broth

½ cup Rice Wine

2 Tablespoons Tamari or GF Soy Sauce

2 Tablespoons Low Sodium Tamari or GF Soy Sauce

¼ cup Rock Sugar or Sugar

3 Green Onions cut in thirds (roots and tips cut off)

3 fresh Ginger slices (about inch 1 x ¼ inch¼-inch each)

1 Star Anise pod or ¼ teaspoon Five Spice Powder

½ Tablespoon Cornstarch mixed with 1 Tablespoon of Water

Place the Pork Belly in a sauté pan (with a lid) and add the Water, Chicken Broth and seasonings. Bring to a boil and return to a simmer, cover and cook for 3 hours. Check occasionally to make sure that there is enough cooking liquid and if necessary, add ¼ cup Water. The Pork Belly is done when it is meltingly tender.

Pull out the Pork Belly pieces and put them in a bowl. Pour off the braising liquid, strain and reserve ½ cup. Freeze the remaining Master Sauce to put in the freezer to use again. Put the ½ cup of Sauce back in the pan. Bring to a boil and then add in the Cornstarch mixture. Stir gently to thicken the sauce and then add the Pork Belly pieces back in and stir to coat.

Variations

- If using to stuff Rou Jia Mo Sandwiches, chop the Pork Belly into small pieces.

- If using Spareribs, split them into individual Ribs and cook them from 1 to 1½ hours depending on how meaty they are.

- If using Chicken Thighs, cook for about one hour.

- If using Chicken Wings, cook for about 30 minutes

- If using Tofu Cubes, marinate them in the sauce first (and use Vegetable Broth if you are making this Vegan) and only cook for 20 minutes.

When you roast fresh Mushrooms, they develop a deeper Umami flavor and a slightly chewier texture that makes them really delicious. We keep the Mushrooms whole if serving as part of an appetizer plate, but cut them up when using them as a filling for Rou Jia Mo Sandwiches or Green Onion Pancake Wraps. We think this is one of the best ways to make Shitake Mushrooms taste even better!

Tamari Roast Mushrooms

2 pounds fresh Shitake Mushrooms
(you can also use Button, Cremini or King Oyster Mushrooms)
⅓ cup Vegetable Oil
½ teaspoon Sea Salt
1 teaspoon Garlic Powder
1 Tablespoon Tamari or GF Soy Sauce

Heat oven to 350 degrees. Wash and dry Mushrooms. Slice off the stems except for King Oyster Mushrooms: just trim the bottom. Then cut into ½ inch slices. And place in a bowl. Mix together the Oil, Salt and Garlic Powder. Add to the Mushrooms and toss to coat. Pour onto a large baking sheet and place in the oven for 20 - 25 minutes, stirring and tossing at least once. Serve as a main dish or use to fill Rou Jia Mo Sandwiches or Green Onion Pancake Wraps.

This is one of my favorite ways to prepare Tofu and it's really simple to make. The Tofu just needs to be marinated overnight and then baked to whatever consistency you like. The longer you bake it, the firmer it becomes. I like it a bit on the softer side. The Tofu soaks up the flavor of the savory marinade and it is delicious! We love it as a filling for Green Onion Pancake Wraps although I sometimes eat it as the main course for dinner with rice and a vegetable. Tofu is so good cooked this way!

Marinated Baked Tofu Slices

1 block of pressed Tofu
¼ cup low sodium Tamari or GF Soy Sauce
¼ cup Rice Wine
1 Tablespoon Rice Vinegar
1 Tablespoon toasted Sesame Oil
1 Tablespoon Honey
1 teaspoon minced Ginger

OPTIONAL
Pieces of Green Onion or Cilantro leaves for garnish

Cut Tofu into 8 slices. Place in a large closing plastic bag. Mix the marinade ingredients in a bowl. Pour over the Tofu. Seal the bag and place in a bowl. Refrigerate and let marinate several hours up to overnight.

Heat oven to 400°F. When ready to cook, place Tofu slices on a rimmed baking pan. Pour over strained marinade. Cook for 15 minutes, turn over and cook for 10–20 minutes more. Serve it as is or sprinkle Green Onion pieces or Cilantro leaves on top. We like to use the Tofu Slices as a filling for Green Onion Pancake Wraps or Rou Jia Mo Sandwiches.

Often called Chinese Tacos, this wonderful dish is usually served as an appetizer in Chinese restaurants. But it has become a favorite lunch or dinner dish for our family, especially during the summer months. It's traditionally made with Squab, but that's a bit difficult to find, so most restaurants and home cooks use Chicken. We make it with both Chicken and Tofu. Mincing the Chicken gives the dish a better texture, but buying the Chicken already ground is definitely a time saver. For the Tofu version, cut the Tofu into small pieces for a better texture. We like to use Butter Lettuce, as the leaves are smaller and make the perfect appetizer size portion. But if you do use another Lettuce, like Iceberg, you will probably need to trim the leaves to a usable size to hold the filling.

Many restaurants, particularly the chains, create highly seasoned Lettuce Wrap fillings, but it is more traditional to keep the flavors of the filling light, so that the drizzled sauce adds the extra flavor punch. We serve it with Hoisin Sauce thinned with Hot Water, a sprinkle of Green Onions and lots of Fried Glass Noodles.

Lettuce Wraps

MINCED CHICKEN AND MUSHROOM FILLING

1 pound minced or ground Chicken

2 Tablespoons Rice Wine

2 Tablespoons Tamari
or GF Soy Sauce

5–6 Dried Shitake Mushrooms, rehydrated in boiling water, stems trimmed and chopped into small pieces – about ½ cup

½ cup chopped Water Chestnuts (from a can)

½ cup minced Green Onion, reserving some of the green tops for garnishing

1 teaspoon peeled and finely minced Ginger

2 Tablespoons Oil

3 Tablespoons Chicken Broth

1 Tablespoon Tamari

⅛ teaspoon toasted Sesame Oil

½ Tablespoon of Cornstarch mixed with 1 Tablespoon of Water

FOR GARNISH

Fried Glass Noodles

Marinate the Chicken with the Rice Wine and 2 Tablespoons of Tamari for at least 15 minutes.

In a small bowl, mix together the Chicken Broth, Tamari and Sesame Oil.

In a large frying pan or wok, heat the Oil and add in the Ginger and the Green Onions. Cook until you smell the fragrance. Then add in the Chicken, Mushrooms and Water Chestnuts and cook until the Chicken is opaque. Add in the sauce mixture. Then add in the Cornstarch and stir until thickened.

Cool slightly before filling the Lettuce.

SAVORY TOFU AND MUSHROOM FILLING

One package of Firm Tofu, cut into small cubes

2 Tablespoons Vegetable Oil

2 cloves of Garlic, minced

5–6 Dried Shitake Mushrooms, rehydrated in boiling water, stems trimmed and chopped into small pieces - about ½ cup

½ cup chopped Water Chestnuts (from a can)

½ cup of minced Green Onions, reserving some of the tops for garnish

1 teaspoon grated Ginger

3 Tablespoons Tamari or GF Soy Sauce

1 Tablespoon Sesame Oil

¼ teaspoon Sugar

FOR GARNISH

Fried Glass Noodles

In a small bowl, mix together the Tamari, Sesame Oil and Sugar.

Dry the Tofu with Paper Towels. Heat Oil in a frying pan and add in the Garlic, Ginger and Green Onions. Cook until you can smell the fragrance. Then add in the Tofu, Mushrooms and Water Chestnuts and cook, stirring frequently until any liquid just starts to dry up and the Tofu starts getting lightly browned. Then pour in the sauce mixture and cook until it is absorbed by the Tofu. Cool slightly before using to the fill the Lettuce.

TO SERVE: Wash 2 heads of Butter Lettuce. Then with the stem side down, hit it against a cutting board to loosen the core and pull it out. Carefully, peel off Lettuce Leaves. Place on a serving plate.

Fill the Lettuce leaves with the filling and sprinkle with reserved Green Onion pieces and fried Glass Noodles. Drizzle with GF Hoisin Sauce thinned with Hot Water.

Spring Rolls are the original Chinese version of what the Western world knows as Egg Rolls. Traditional Spring Roll wrappers are light and delicate, even when deep-fried, whereas as Egg Roll wrappers are thicker and more substantial. We always had Spring Rolls at Chinese New Year as they are considered a lucky food and I always loved them! I had to give them up when I stopped eating wheat. Then I found out that the Vietnamese use Rice Paper as wrappers for their version of Egg Rolls and we started using them instead.

The big difference is that we bake them instead of deep-frying them. For those of you who are used to the texture of Egg Rolls made with wheat flour, these won't be quite as crispy. They will be only lightly crisp and a little bit chewy too. They are delicious in their own way and such a joy for those of us who are trying to avoid gluten and still want to enjoy Asian snacks. We've also included a recipe for making little mini Rice Paper Triangles using round Rice Paper that makes a great appetizer for parties.

Baked Rice Paper Spring Rolls

1 package of Square Rice Wrappers - you will need between 12 – 18 (depending on how big you make them)

1 recipe of Filling

2 Tablespoons Vegetable Oil

Heat the oven to 425°F.

Take one wrapper at a time and place it under running cold tap Water or dip into a shallow pan filled with Water. Place the Rice Paper on a plate or cutting board with the points facing up and down and out to the right and left, like a diamond. Put ⅓ – ½ cup of cooked filling slightly below center and roll the bottom point up and over the filling. Pull in each side, tucking it tightly and roll all the way up. The rolls should be about 3 inches long.

Put the rolls directly onto a baking sheet covered with a silicone liner or parchment paper. Brush each Spring Roll with Oil and place on the pan, oiled-side down. It is important to make sure that you space them far enough apart so that they do not touch! Then brush the tops with oil. Bake for 20–25 minutes. The Spring Rolls should be lightly browned. Remove carefully with a spatula.

Mini Rice Paper Triangles

15–18 Round Rice Paper Wrappers
1 recipe of Filling
2 Tablespoons Vegetable Oil

Heat the oven to 425°F.

Fill a shallow dish with water and place one sheet of Rice Paper in it. Remove and cut the Rice Paper in half with Kitchen Shears. Take one piece at a time and place the flat edge away from you. Fill with 1 heaping Tablespoon of filling in the center. Pull down one side over the filling and then pull down the other side to make a point. Then take the bottom rounded open edge and turn upward to make a triangle. Pinch tightly and turn over. Then place on a silicone liner or parchment covered baking sheet and brush with Oil.

Cook for 10 minutes. Remove the baking sheet from the oven and turn the Triangles over. Brush with the remaining Oil. Cook for an additional 10 minutes or until crisp and lightly browned. Serve with the dipping sauce of your choice.

Egg Rolls are a Western invention made with a much thicker wheat wrapper than is used for Spring Rolls. They are filled just like Spring Rolls, but are usually bigger and heartier. No one really knows why they are called Egg Rolls as there is no Egg in the wrapper or in the filling. The trick for making Gluten Free Egg Rolls is to use Tofu Skins, which mimic the wheat wrappers perfectly. We advise that you rehydrate more Tofu Skins than you need since they tear easily. The extras can be used to patch any holes in the Egg Rolls when you are rolling them, or they can be cut into strips and fried to make Tofu Skin Threads. If you are craving Egg Rolls, this recipe is for you!

Fried Tofu Skin Egg Rolls

20 Tofu Skins (Bean Curd Sheets), soaked in warm water until soft

Drain and cut the Tofu Skins into 12-inch squares. Using one Sheet at a time, put a Tofu Skin on a cutting board with one of the points facing you. Place about ¼ cup of filling in the lower center and pull up the point closest to you to wrap over the filling. Then pull in both sides tightly and continue rolling.

Place the Egg Rolls seam side down on a baking sheet and continue until all wrappers are used. If a wrapper tears, use a scrap piece to cover the hole (from the inside) and reroll.

Heat 4 cups of Oil in a wok or a deep fryer until it reaches 375°F. Drop the Egg Rolls in two at a time into the hot oil and cook until bubbled and browned. Remove to a paper towel covered plate until all Egg Rolls are cooked.

They can be kept warm in a 200°F oven and they reheat well in a 350°F oven.

This recipe is from an Indonesian friend of mine, who is of Chinese descent. Many years ago, her Mother was making these while I was visiting and they were so good that I couldn't stop eating them! The combination of shredded Chicken, Jicama, Onion and Bean Sprouts makes a delicious filling for Egg Rolls or Spring Rolls. Jicama, which is called Yam Bean in China adds a delightful crunch. Egg Rolls or Spring Rolls made with this filling are especially good with any of the sweet or spicy dipping sauces.

Chicken, Jicama and Bean Sprout Filling

4 cups cooked poached Chicken

1 medium Jicama, peeled and cut into julienne
pieces about 1½ inches long

1 medium Onion, sliced thin and cut into about 1½ inch lengths

2 handfuls of Bean Sprouts (about 2 cups), washed

2 Tablespoons Vegetable Oil

2 teaspoons Salt

⅛ teaspoon fresh ground Black Pepper

Shred chicken and then cut into about 1½ inch lengths. In a large frying pan, heat the 2 Tablespoons of Oil. Put in the Onions and Jicama and cook until softened. Add in the Bean Sprouts and Chicken and cook until the Bean Sprouts are hot. Season with Salt and Pepper and stir to combine.

Refrigerate to cool before using as a filling for Spring Rolls or Egg Rolls.

Makes 15 – 18

This is the classic filling for Spring Rolls or Egg Rolls from my Mother, made from a variety of vegetables along with Shitake Mushrooms and Glass Noodles. We sometimes add Meat or Tofu, and Bean Sprouts are a particularly good addition, as is Bok Choy. You just need to have about 6 to 8 cups of cooked filling. Make sure that you cook the vegetables only until they begin soften so that they don't overcook once they are inside the wrappers. Spring Rolls or Egg Rolls made with this filling taste especially good with the savory and spicy dipping sauces.

Classic Vegetable Filling

4 cups of Napa Cabbage leaves, trimmed and cut into strips

5 Green Onions, cut into slivers about 1½-inches long

2 Carrots, peeled and sliced into slivers about 1½-inches long

6 Shitake Mushrooms, rehydrated and sliced into thin strips

2–4 ounces of Glass Noodles, soaked in
hot water for 20–30 minutes

3 Tablespoons Tamari or GF Soy Sauce

½ teaspoon White Pepper

3 Tablespoons Vegetable Oil

OPTIONAL

1–2 cups thin sliced cooked Pork, Chicken or Tofu

2 handfuls (about 2 cups) of fresh Bean Sprouts

Drain the Glass Noodles and cut them into 1½ inch lengths. Put aside.

Heat a wok and put in the 3 Tablespoons of Vegetable Oil. Add in the Green Onions, Carrots and Napa Cabbage and any other vegetables you are using. Stir-fry until the Cabbage just starts to wilt, but is still crunchy. Add in the Mushrooms and Glass Noodles along with the Tamari and White Pepper. Toss and stir until well mixed. Take off the heat and put the mixture into a large bowl. Cool slightly and then refrigerate until completely cool before using to fill wrappers.

This is a popular Dim Sum dish whose real name is Lo Mai Gai. It has always been one of my favorites. For me, it was like opening a savory and delicious present, as it is studded with different meats or vegetables. The unique aroma of steamed Lotus leaves is something that simply can't be described, but they give the filling a subtle, enticing scent.

I got brave a number of years ago and started making them myself mostly because I wanted to be sure that they didn't have any dried shrimp in them. I discovered that they are really very easy. The only time-consuming part is gathering and cooking some of the filling ingredients. I learned a trick from my Auntie Pearl and that is to add Soy Sauce, or in this case, Tamari to the Rice soaking liquid. This ensures that the Rice has more flavor built in. You can certainly make these Vegan if you like or you can add in several kinds of meat. When you make them yourself, it is your choice as to what you put in. You can also wrap these in parchment paper, but it is worth sourcing the dried Lotus Leaves at an Asian market or online just for the special fragrance that infuses the Sticky Rice.

Sticky Rice Wrapped in Lotus Leaves

2 cups Sticky Rice (Short Grain White Rice)

3 cups Water for Soaking + 2 Tablespoons Tamari or GF Soy Sauce

3 dried Lotus Leaves, cut in half Water for Soaking

8–10 Dried Shitake Mushrooms (depending on their size)

RICE SEASONING

2 Tablespoons Vegetable Oil

1 small Shallot, minced

3 Green Onions, trimmed sliced into small pieces

1 Tablespoon Rice Wine

2 Tablespoons Mushroom Tamari

Soak Rice in room temperature Water and Tamari for at least 2 hours, preferably overnight. Soak Lotus Leaves in the sink or a large pot for one hour and then cut in half with kitchen shears. Soak Shitake Mushrooms in Boiling

Water to cover for at least 20 minutes. When Mushrooms are softened, trim off the stem and cut into quarters.

Drain the Rice. In a large frying pan or Wok, heat the Oil and add in the Shallot pieces, the Mushroom pieces and the Green Onions. Cook until soft. Then add in the Rice, the Rice Wine and the Mushroom Tamari and toss to coat. Remove to a bowl and let cool.

Makes 6

MARINATED CHICKEN FILLING

½ pound of Chicken Thighs, cut into small pieces
1 teaspoon Tamari or GF Soy Sauce
1 teaspoon Rice Wine
½ teaspoon Cornstarch
1 Tablespoon Oil

Marinate the Chicken in Tamari, Rice Wine and Cornstarch for 15 minutes.

Heat the Oil in a frying pan and add in the Chicken. Cook until the Chicken becomes opaque. Remove and put the Chicken pieces onto a plate to cool.

OTHER OPTIONAL FILLING INGREDIENTS

6 Water Chestnuts (from a can) cut in half
6 roasted Chestnuts, cut in half
⅔ cup cooked Lotus Seeds
¼ cup of Bamboo Shoot slices (fresh or from a can) cut in bite size pieces
1 cup of Chinese Bacon Bits, uncooked
6–1-inch pieces of Braised Pork Belly
3 Salted Duck Egg Yolks, cut in half

TO WRAP: Take one Lotus Leaf half and lay it flat on a cutting board. Take ⅓ cup of the Rice Mixture and place in the center. Put any of the filling ingredients on top. Take another ⅓ cup of the Rice Mixture and pour on top of the filling. The Rice does not need to cover the filling completely. Take the four sides of the Lotus Leaf and wrap into a tight rectangle around the filling. Repeat with the remaining Lotus Leaves.

Place each Lotus Leaf packet seam side down in a steamer. Steam for 1½ hours. If you have any leftovers, you can wrap them in plastic wrap and store in the refrigerator. To reheat, steam for an additional 30 minutes or place in the microwave covered with a wet paper towel until hot.

CHAPTER 10

Chinese Vegetables & Sweets

This was one of my Father's favorite dishes, so my Grandfather and my Mother made it often for him. It's a really simple stir-fry with a light sweet and sour sauce that somehow magically combines with the lightly caramelized Cabbage to make something much more than the parts. Use the Cornstarch if you prefer the sauce to cling to the Cabbage for more flavor. This dish is quick and easy to make and it's just so good. Everyone in our family loves Cabbage cooked this way!

Sweet and Sour Cabbage

½ large Green Head Cabbage
2 Tablespoons Vegetable Oil
½ teaspoon Salt
Pinch of White Pepper
2 Tablespoons Water

2 Tablespoons Sugar
2 Tablespoons Tamari
or GF Soy Sauce
2 Tablespoons Rice Vinegar
Optional ½ teaspoon Cornstarch
mixed with 1 teaspoon Water

In a small bowl, mix together the sauce by combining the Water, Sugar, Tamari and Rice Vinegar.

Cut the Cabbage in half and then cut off the core. Then cut into about 1-inch pieces. Heat a wok or frying pan and add in the 2 Tablespoons of Vegetable Oil. Then add in the Cabbage and sprinkle with Salt and Pepper. Stir-fry, tossing often until all the Cabbage is coated with Oil. Cook until the edges of the Cabbage just begin to brown. Continue to toss and then pour in the sauce mixture and stir to coat the Cabbage. Add the Cornstarch mixture, if using, and stir to combine. Serve warm or at room temperature.

One of the frequently asked questions I get in my cooking classes is how to make Stir Fried Greens taste like the ones from a Chinese Restaurant. It's really simple and there are only a few tricks that will make your Greens shine! First, you need to slice some Garlic. This is to get the maximum Garlic flavor into the Oil and the larger size will keep the Garlic from burning. Second, wet the Greens again even after you wash them, right before you put them into a wok or frying pan, as you need that extra moisture to get the right texture and keep the Greens from burning. Sprinkle with a pinch of Salt and a pinch of Sugar. This is a very import-ant step for balancing out the natural bitterness of Greens. Then add a small amount of Chicken or Vegetable Broth. And lastly, add a few drops of toasted Sesame Oil at the end for the fragrance that adds so much to the dish. After only a few minutes of cooking, you have made delicious Chinese restaurant-quality Chinese Style Greens at home.

Chinese Style Sautéed Greens

1 large bunch of Chinese Greens (Amaranth, Bok Choy, Choy Sum or Yu Choy. You can also use Chard or Spinach)

2 Tablespoons Vegetable Oil

2–3 large Garlic cloves, peeled and sliced thin

1–2 Tablespoons Vegetable Oil (use less if using a nonstick skillet)

⅛ teaspoon Salt

⅛ teaspoon of Sugar

¼ cup Chicken or Vegetable Broth

¼ teaspoon toasted Sesame Oil

Cut off the bottom part of the greens and cut into bite size pieces. Be sure to cut the stem part into smaller pieces than the leaves. Place in a colander and wash.

Then heat Oil in a wok or frying pan until hot. Add the Garlic and cook until the Garlic fragrance rises, stirring often. Re-wet the Greens in a colander and give it a shake before you put them into the pan. Then add the Greens to the hot pan. It should sizzle a lot. Sprinkle the Greens with the Salt and Sugar and push and turn the Greens with a spatula until it wilts. Add the Broth and the few drops of Sesame Oil and cook until it almost evaporates (this will happen fast) and then put on a plate to serve.

This was my Mother's way of making Eggplant. When we asked her how to make it, she just gave us the ingredients, so it took us a while to get the right amounts of everything. Now we make it all the time and we all love it!

Shanghai Style Eggplant

1½ pounds Chinese or Japanese Eggplant

¼ cup Vegetable Oil

1-inch chunk of Ginger, peeled and grated

3 Green Onions, trimmed and cut into small pieces (reserve some to green pieces for garnish)

2 Garlic cloves, minced

¼ cup Rice Wine

2 Tablespoons Tamari or GF Soy Sauce

2 Tablespoons Chicken or Vegetable Broth

1 teaspoon Sugar

Trim the Eggplants and cut into 1-inch chunks. Heat the Oil in a wok. Add in the Eggplant and cook until the Eggplant is soft and just starting to brown. Then add in the Ginger, Green Onions and Garlic. Cook until you smell the fragrance. Then add in the Rice Wine, Tamari, Broth and Sugar. Cook and continue to stir until most of the liquid is absorbed.

Pour onto a serving plate and sprinkle with the reserved Green Onion pieces.

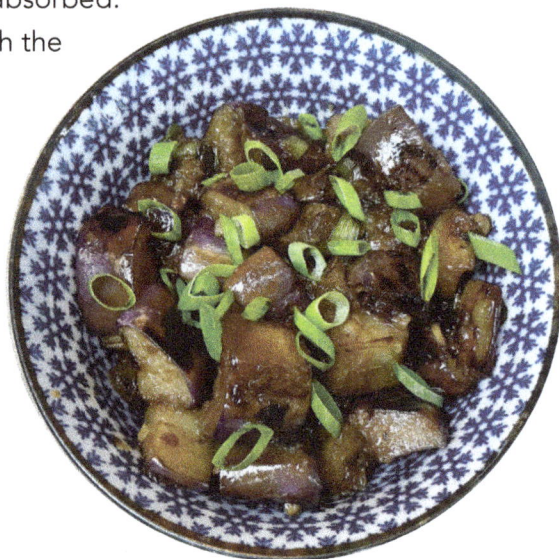

Gai Lan, also known as Chinese Broccoli, is served at Dim Sum Restaurants around the world. They usually cook it right at the table by dunking it in a pot of boiling water on their cart. It is blanched only briefly and then drizzled with Oyster Sauce. This is our version served with our homemade Vegan Oyster Sauce that we call Mushroom Tamari.

Gai Lan Dim Sum Style

1 bunch of Gai Lan, washed, bottom ½ inch of the bottom stem cut off

3 Tablespoons Mushroom Tamari

1 teaspoon Sugar

In a large pot, heat about 4 inches of water until it comes to a boil. Drop in the Gai Lan and reduce heat and cook for 3 minutes. Remove the Gai Lan from the water with tongs and place on a large serving platter. Mix together the Mushroom Tamari and Sugar and pour the sauce over the Gai Lan. Serve immediately.

This is our new favorite way of making Gai Lan. When you roast it, the leaves become a bit crisp which make them a bit like Kale Chips, while the stalks get tender. We drizzle a little bit of Sweet Tamari over it. We usually have to triple the amount because everyone loves it so much!

Roasted Gai Lan with Sweet Tamari Drizzle

1 bunch of Gai Lan, washed, bottom ¼-inch of stalk cut off
3 Tablespoons Vegetable Oil
¼ teaspoon Sea Salt
3 Tablespoons Sweet Tamari

Heat the oven to 425°F. Peel the bottom stalks of the Gai Lan with a vegetable peeler. Drizzle 2 Tablespoons of Oil on a large sheet pan. Place the Gai Lan down and drizzle the top of the Gai Lan with the remaining 1 Tablespoon of Oil. Sprinkle with Salt. Place in the oven and let roast for 15 minutes. If the leaves are crispy, it's done. If not, leave in for an additional 5 minutes. Put Gai Lan on a serving tray and drizzle the Sweet Tamari all over in a thin stream. Serve immediately.

This is our family's favorite way of cooking Green Beans. It's like Dry Fried String Beans except the Green Beans are blanched instead of being deep-fried. This leaves them with more snap, although you can cook them longer if you like them softer. It's a very simple preparation with a lot more flavor than you would expect. Our friends frequently request this recipe and we make it often.

Garlic Green Beans

1 pound Green Beans, ends snapped or cut off
3 cloves of Garlic minced fine
1 Tablespoon Tamari or GF Soy Sauce
2 Tablespoons Vegetable Oil
⅛ teaspoon Sugar
⅛ teaspoon Salt
⅛ teaspoon toasted Sesame Oil

Put enough water in a pot large enough to hold the Green Beans and bring the water to a boil. Put in the Green Beans and cook for 4 minutes or until the Green Beans are barely tender. Drain and rinse with cold water. You could also steam them for 5–6 minutes instead.

Heat a wok or large frying pan and add in the Oil. Then add in the Green Beans (the Oil should sizzle) and stir for 1–2 minutes. The Green Beans should brown slightly. Then add in the Garlic, the Sugar and the Salt and stir-fry for another minute. Pour in the Tamari. Keep stirring until the Tamari is almost evaporated and drizzle in the Sesame Oil. Toss to coat. Serve immediately.

Sugar Snap Peas are one of our favorite vegetables. They are crisp and sweet and need very little cooking. When you have been busy making other dishes, this dish comes together in a matter of minutes and it's simply delicious!

Sesame Sugar Snap Peas

1 pound of Sugar Snap Peas, ends snipped off and strings pulled
¼ teaspoon Sea Salt
1 Tablespoon toasted Sesame Oil
OPTIONAL
1 teaspoon Toasted Sesame Seeds

Bring a small pot of water to a boil and put in the Sugar Snap Peas. Cook for 2 minutes and test. Cook for no longer than 1–2 minutes more. The Peas should be just barely tender and still crisp. Drain in a colander and immediately rinse with cold water. Put into a serving bowl and sprinkle with Salt and Sesame Oil. Then sprinkle on Sesame Seeds, if using, toss and serve. This dish is also good served cold.

Pineapple Cake is actually a traditional Taiwanese Cookie that has a Pineapple filling inside. It was so valued that a box of these used to be given as wedding gifts and as presents for Chinese New Year. My Aunt Pearl, who lived in Taiwan, used to bring them whenever she visited and I always loved them. I really wanted to create a Gluten Free version. We found that it was difficult to create a filled cookie, so we changed the recipe into cookie bars with a tender shortbread base and top and we like it even better! We use Lard as that is traditional, but you can use Vegetable Shortening to make it Vegan. And if you are only avoiding Lactose, it's delicious made with Ghee. Strangely, it is much better with canned Pineapple than fresh, as the Pineapple flavor is much richer. It's a cookie that is so good that no one ever suspects that it is actually Gluten Free!

Taiwanese Pineapple Bars

SHORTBREAD LAYER

2 cups Gluten Free Flour Blend with Xanthan Gum
(See recipe on page 27)
1 cup Lard, Vegetable Shortening or Ghee

½ **cup Sugar**
¼ **teaspoon Salt**
½ **teaspoon Baking Powder**

Lightly grease a 9 x 9-inch pan.

Blend the Lard (Vegetable Shortening or Ghee) and Sugar together in a food processor or stand mixer until creamy. Then add in the GF Flour, Salt and Baking Powder and mix until the mixture becomes a soft dough.

PINEAPPLE FILLING

1 20-oz can unsweetened crushed Pineapple, drained, reserve Pineapple Juice
1 8-oz can unsweetened canned Pineapple, drained, reserve Pineapple Juice
¼ – ⅓ cup Brown Rock Sugar or Brown Sugar

¼ cup Golden Syrup (you can also use Corn Syrup or Zuckerrubensirup)
2 teaspoons Cornstarch mixed with 1 Tablespoon of Water

In a large frying pan with high sides, put in the Pineapple, the ½ cup of Pineapple Juice, the Sugar and the Golden Syrup. Cook on medium heat, stirring often until the liquid is nearly all evaporated, about 20 – 25 minutes and the Pineapple mixture is a light golden brown. Then add in the Cornstarch mixture and cook for 1 minute until thickened. Cool until ready to use.

TO MAKE THE BARS: Heat the oven to 350°F and grease an 9 x 9-inch square pan.

Take ½ of the Shortbread Dough and press down into the prepared pan with wet hands. Then add the Pineapple Filling, smoothing it with a back of a spoon to the edges. Then take the remaining Shortbread Dough and roll out a little at a time and cut into small circles, squares or triangles. Place on top of the Pineapple mixture and cover the filling as much as possible.

Bake for about 45 – 50 minutes or until the top is light golden brown and the Pineapple Filling is bubbling. Cool and then cut into squares.

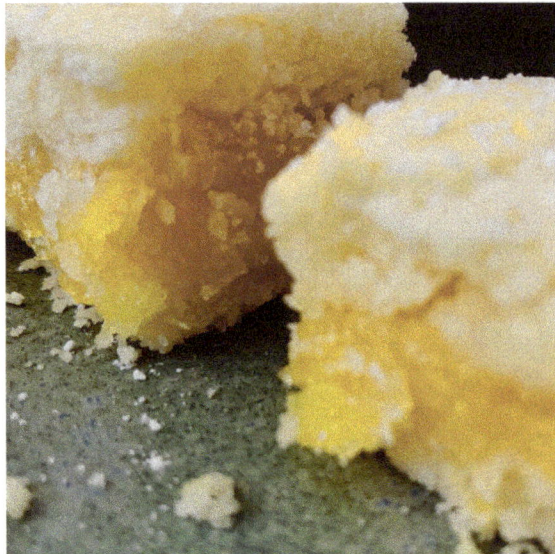

Lychees are an amazing fruit with a wonderful perfumed fragrance and a delicate sweet taste. They are a very seasonal fruit and they are often hard to find, but luckily the canned version of this fruit is also delicious. Everyone in my family loves Lychees in any form. I used to buy my kids big plastic containers of individually wrapped Lychee Jellies that had one Nata de Coco cube within like a prize. I realized that I could make them quite easily myself using canned Lychees, although you can also use Lychee Juice. You actually use the Syrup, Nata de Coco cubes (sometimes found already Lychee flavored) and Gelatin. You can easily substitute Agar Agar to make a Vegan version and the only difference will be that the Jelly will turn out firmer.

We like to use lots of Nata de Coco cubes and we always add a bit of Lemon Juice to brighten the flavor. We like to make the Jelly a bit on the harder side, but you can certainly make the Jelly softer by adding less Gelatin and set it in small bowls or even all together in a big bowl. We serve Lychee Jelly cut into cubes and piled up in a bowl or plate with the reserved Lychees surrounding them. We think Lychee Jelly will surprise you!

Lychee Jelly

1 20-oz can of Lychees in Heavy Syrup or 1½ cups of Lychee Juice

1 packet of unflavored Gelatin or 2 teaspoons Agar Agar Powder

½ cup or more of Nata de Coco cubes in Syrup

½ Tablespoon fresh Lemon Juice

Drain the Syrup from the Lychees into a measuring cup. There should be approximately 1½ cups. Place the Lychees in a container and pour in ½ cup of to keep them moistened. Refrigerate them until it is time to serve.

IF YOU ARE USING GELATIN: Take the ½ cup of the Lychee Syrup from the measuring cup and pour it into a mixing bowl. Add in the Gelatin and Lemon Juice and whisk to combine. Pour the remaining ½ cup of Syrup into a small saucepan and heat until it comes to a boil. Take the pan off the heat and add the Hot Syrup to the Gelatin mixture.

IF YOU ARE USING AGAR AGAR: Pour ½ cup of Syrup into a mixing bowl and add the Lemon Juice. Pour the remaining Syrup into a small saucepan and mix in the Agar Agar, whisking to combine thoroughly. Heat until the mixture comes to a boil and then add to the Syrup in the mixing bowl.

TO SET THE JELLY: Evenly distribute the Nata de Coco cubes in a small rectangular or square container. Pour the Lychee Jelly mixture over the cubes carefully. Cover and put in the refrigerator for several hours or overnight.

FOR SERVING: Cut the Lychee Jelly into cubes and put into a bowl or on a plate and surround them with the reserved Lychees or serve individual bowls with Lychees piled on top.

Traditionally, this Southern Chinese dessert is made more like a soup than a pudding and it usually contains Milk. My kids rebelled at dessert soup and they wanted a pudding that was thicker and creamer. I wanted one that was Lactose Free and this was the result. We offer you a Vegan version too. It's traditionally topped with Melon, but my kids always wanted it served with Strawberries or Raspberries and I like mine topped with Mango. This is a delicious thick and creamy pudding, but be sure to wait unitl right before serving to add the fruit.

Coconut Tapioca Pudding with Fruit

⅔ cup quick cooking Tapioca Pearls
2 14-oz cans full-fat Coconut Milk
(or substitute 1½ cans low-fat
Coconut Milk + 2 Eggs)
¼ teaspoon Salt
½ cup Sugar
1 Egg lightly beaten

OPTIONAL
½ teaspoon Vanilla
2 cup diced Honeydew Melon,
Cantaloupe, Mango, Strawberries
or Raspberries

Soak the tapioca in hot tap water for 30 minutes. Drain the Tapioca and then mix the Tapioca, Sugar, Salt and Coconut Milk in a pot and bring to a boil over medium-high heat. Reduce the heat to medium-low, and simmer for 10 minutes, stirring often.

Put the Egg into a mixing bowl. Whisk in about ½ cup of the hot Tapioca mixture into the Egg Mixture, a little at a time to temper it. Then put the Egg Mixture into the rest of the Tapioca in the pot. Stir to combine thoroughly. Reduce heat to low and simmer gently for 5 more minutes, stirring constantly. Then remove from the heat and ladle into small serving bowls. Serve either warm or chilled. Refrigerate if not serving immediately. Top with the fruit right before serving.

TO MAKE VEGAN VERSION: Leave out the Egg and add in 2 Tablespoons of Cornstarch mixed with ¼ cup of Water at the same point in the recipe where the Egg is added. Cook until thickened.

Mango Pudding is a classic Dim Sum Sweet but we needed to make one without Milk or Cream, so we created one using Coconut Milk or Soy Milk instead. To make it a bit more interesting, we also added some juice from a Mandarin Orange (Tangerine) and some zest from the peel as well. Be sure to zest it first before juicing it! The color of fresh Mangoes varies from yellow to dark orange. We like to use the Yellow Ataulfo Mangoes as they are often available to us, but any Mangoes make a delicious Mandarin Mango Pudding!

Mandarin Mango Pudding

2 cups Pureed fresh, frozen or canned Mango

2 packages Gelatin or 2–3 teaspoons Agar Agar*

¼ cup fresh squeezed Mandarin Orange Juice

1 cup full fat Coconut Milk (or Soy Milk)

¼ cup Sugar (White for more delicate taste and Brown Sugar for a deeper taste. Don't use Sugar if you use canned Mangos in Syrup)

Zest of one Mandarin Orange, divided

In a mixing bowl, add in ½ cup Cocnut Milk or Soy Milk, the pureed Mango, the Mandarin Orange Juice, Sugar and ½ teaspoon Zest. Stir to combine and then sprinkle on the Gelatin, using a whisk to incorporate it.

In a small pot, heat ½ cup of the Coconut Milk or Soy Milk until boiling and add to the Mango mixture. Whisk to combine. Pour into 6 ramekins or custard cups and sprinkle with the remaining Zest and refrigerate until firm.*If using Agar Agar, mix in with the Coconut Milk or Soy Milk and bring to a boil. Then proceed with the recipel

As a child, I got to have Egg Custard Tarts when we went out for Dim Sum. When I eventually had Custard Pies anywhere else, I thought everyone was copying the Chinese. It turns out that in fact, the Chinese were influenced by the Portuguese in Macau and by the English in Guangdong. Egg Tarts are traditionally made with Condensed Milk, but we substitute Soy Milk or Coconut Milk and it turns out wonderfully every time. We like to make them bigger, using a cupcake tin rather than putting them in small tart pans. With a Gluten Free Pie Crust as a base, you never have to go without these delicious Egg Custard Tarts again!

Dim Sum Egg Custard Tarts

FOR CRUST

1¼ cup Gluten-Free Flour Blend
(See recipe on page 27)

2 Tablespoons Sugar

½ teaspoon Sea Salt

8 Tablespoons Lard
or Vegetable Shortening

⅓ cup Ice Water
+ 1 – 2 Tablespoons more

Mix together all the dry ingredients. Then add in the Lard or Shortening with a pastry cutter or in a food processor until it incorporates completely. Then add in ⅓ cup of Ice Water and mix to combine. If the mixture is too dry, add in the additional Water, 1 Tablespoon at a time. Let the dough rest in the refrigerator for 15 minutes. Then cut into 12 equal pieces. Roll each piece of dough in to a ball. Sprinkle a cutting board with a little Rice Flour and roll the dough into approximately a 4-inch circle. Place into an oiled cupcake tin pressing down lightly. Cut around the opening leaving ¼ inch for crimping the edges. Add the extra pastry dough back to the bowl. Repeat until all the tins are lined with pastry. Then crimp the edges of each tart and heat the oven to 375°F.

FOR CUSTARD

8 Egg Yolks
2 cups Soy Milk or Coconut Milk
⅓–½ cup Sugar (depending
on how sweet you like it)
a pinch of Salt

OPTIONAL

¼ teaspoon Vanilla Extract

Whisk the Eggs, Sugar, Salt and Soy Milk or Coconut Milk together in a small saucepan. Heat over medium heat until the mixture just starts to bubble. Remove from the heat.

TO BAKE: Pour the Egg mixture into the pastry shells carefully. Place the cupcake tin on a baking sheet in the middle of the oven. Bake for 20 minutes and turn the heat down to 350°F and continue to cook for another 10 minutes or until the pastry crust is browned and the custard is just set. The filling will look soft. Cool the Egg Custard Tarts before removing from the cupcake tin.

Makes 12

I remember being so excited whenever Toffee Apples and Bananas would arrive at the end of a Chinese Banquet. Of course, we were all so full by that time that it was hard to eat more than a few pieces, but we did try because they were so good. The Chinese have always candied fruit and somewhere along the line, they started dipping the fruit in a batter before glazing them, making them more like fritters. We simplified the recipe so that you coat the fruit pieces in Cornstarch before frying them quickly and then coating them in the Toffee Syrup. Stephen introduced our version at the restaurant where he worked and they were a big hit!

Toffee Apples and Bananas

FOR THE FRIED APPLES AND BANANAS

4 Apples, cored, peeled and cut into chunks

4 slightly under-ripe Bananas, peeled and cut into chunks

1⅓ cup of Cornstarch

Oil for deep-frying to a depth of 2-inches

Heat the Oil in the wok or in a deep fryer to about 350°F.

Put the Cornstarch in a large, sealing plastic bag. Drop in some of the Apple and Banana pieces and shake to coat with Cornstarch. Drop about 4 to 5 pieces of fruit at a time into the hot Oil. Cook the Apple and Banana pieces until they are golden brown, about 5 to 6 minutes. Drain on a paper-towel lined plate. Place in a bowl and pour the Syrup over.

FOR TOFFEE GLAZE

1 cup Sugar

2 Tablespoons Oil

¼ cup Water

a pinch of Salt

⅓ cup Sesame Seeds

When you put the fruit in to be fried, heat the Oil in a small saucepan and add the Sugar, Salt and Water. Stir until blended. Bring to a boil and reduce heat. Cook until the Sugar Syrup is a very light golden-brown color, about 10 minutes. Add Sesame Seeds and remove from heat and then pour over the fruit. Don't wait or the Syrup will harden. Toss the fruit with a spoon, let cool and then remove individual pieces to a serving plate one at a time.

Tofu Pudding is a classic Chinese dessert made with Soft Tofu covered in a sweet syrup, usually made with either Brown Sugar or Ginger. I'm partial to the Ginger version, but I have to admit that I got to eat this most often as a child when I had a stomachache, as Ginger is so good for your digestion. We updated the traditional recipe by adding in a pinch of Salt to make the flavor a bit more complex and serving it with the Ginger chunks instead of straining them out, for some bright pops of caramelized Ginger flavor. You can easily double the Syrup to add in more if you like it sweeter. It's a wonderful and unusual dessert and if you have any extra syrup, it also makes a great mixer for drinks.

Tofu Pudding with Ginger Syrup

1 cup Water
½ cup Rock Sugar
¼ teaspoon flaky Sea Salt
1 – 2-inch chunk of Ginger, peeled and cut into a small dice
2 11-oz packages of Soon Tofu or Soft Tofu

Put the Water, Rock Sugar, Salt and Ginger into a small saucepan Bring to a boil over medium heat, stirring to melt the Sugar. Turn down to a simmer and cook for an additional 15 minutes, stirring often. The Ginger Syrup should reduce and turn a very light golden-brown color.

Remove the Tofu from the package and cut into half and then ¼-inch slices if using Soon Tofu or into 1-inch chunks if using Soft Tofu. Place the Tofu carefully in the serving bowl using a spatula.

Pour the Ginger Syrup over the Tofu. Cover and place in the refrigerator to let the flavor permeate the Tofu before serving.

Index

www.ingramcontent.com/pod-product-compliance
Lightning Source LLC
Chambersburg PA
CBHW040255100426
42811CB00011B/1272